DR. TOM MALONE

PREACHES ON

SALVATION

DR. TOM MALONE

PREACHES ON

SALVATION

SWORD of the LORD PUBLISHERS

P. O. BOX 1099, MURFREESBORO, TN 37133

Printed and Bound in the United States of America

Table of Contents

Introduction

Introduction

I only presume to publish these simple sermons because God so wonderfully blessed them when preached at Emmanuel Baptist Church in years gone by.

In those wonderful days hundreds were saved by preaching such simple Bible sermons about Jesus and salvation. God has always honored the preaching of the cross and sermons which encourage lost sinners to come to Christ and be saved.

We should be busy daily getting sinners saved. Teaching and studying theology must not take the place of preaching evangelistic gospel sermons to the unsaved. It was such a simple gospel sermon by a precious country preacher that brought me to Christ August 12, 1935.

Jesus said, "Go ye into all the world, and preach the *gospel*."

Dr. Tom Malone, Sr.
1995

Chapter I

Dying in Sin—Lost Forever

First Prize-Winning Sermon in Sword
Evangelistic Sermon Contest, 1960

"Then said Jesus again unto them, I go my way, and ye shall seek me, and shall die in your sins: whither I go, ye cannot come."—John 8:21.

"I said therefore unto you, that ye shall die in your sins: for if ye believe not that I am he, ye shall die in your sins."—John 8:24.

Beyond any shadow of doubt, Jesus speaks here of the worst tragedy that could possibly befall a human being—the loss of the soul, the tragedy of not knowing the Son of God as Saviour, of missing Heaven and going to Hell. When Jesus said, "Whither I go, ye cannot come," He spoke of the eternal separation of a lost soul from a pure and compassionate Saviour who died for the sins of the world. He referred to that impassable gulf between Heaven and Hell across which no human can ever go.

What soul-searching and tragic words these are, "I go my way, and ye shall seek me, and shall die in your sins: whither I go, ye cannot come." The loss of health or wealth or reputation pales into insignificance in comparison to the tragic loss of the human soul. Oh, soul out of Christ, give ear to the divine portrayal of life's greatest tragedy as recorded in this chapter.

These people were lost in spite of their religion. They certainly were not without religious ritual and form and ceremony. They were well schooled in all the Mosaic teachings. They had a religious background, their forebearers for many centuries being known as God's peculiar people.

However, like millions today, they substituted religion for regeneration, ritual for righteousness and human tradition for divine commandment. They were lost; worse yet, they were so blind and prejudiced and so steeped in unscriptural religion that even Jesus held out no hope for them.

Paul well described them in Romans 10:3, "For they being ignorant of God's righteousness, and going about to establish their own righteousness, have not submitted themselves unto the righteousness of God." No wonder Jesus said, "Ye...shall die in your sins: whither I go, ye cannot come."

They were lost in spite of the nearness of Jesus. They had heard Him forgive the sins of the adulterous woman, saying, "Neither do I condemn thee: go, and sin no more." They had heard His offer of Heaven's light for earth's darkness: "I am the light of the world: he that followeth me shall not walk in darkness, but shall have the light of life" (John 8:12).

He had come to them from the Father and worked miracles of love and had spoken words of grace which bore witness to His deity. He had offered them freedom from the slavery of sin: "If the Son therefore shall make you free, ye shall be free indeed" (John 8:36). Yes, the blessed Saviour was nearer than their breath, yet they refused Him; worse yet, they sought to stone Him!

In view of their indignation against Him, their hatred, their depravity, their sin, He said, "Ye...shall die in your sins: whither I go, ye cannot come." They were lost in spite of such wonderful access to the truth.

These people were not Gentiles to whom the Gospel had never been preached. They were not of nations sitting in darkness to whom no light had ever come. They were not of remote lands into whose language the sweetest gospel story had never been translated! Rather, they were a favored people. God had spoken to them, the Living Word had walked in and out among them, yet they were lost! Jesus told them, "Ye shall know the truth, and the truth shall make you free." They despised the truth, rejected the light and gambled with their souls.

Why did they refuse the Son of God as Saviour and Friend? Why is it that millions of our generation die in sin and are forever cut off from Christ and Heaven?

I. PEOPLE DIE IN SIN BECAUSE OF UNBELIEF

Jesus said to His audience, "And because I tell you the truth, ye believe me not. Which of you convinceth me of sin? And if I say the truth, why do ye not believe me?" (John 8:45, 46).

Unbelief is the most horrible and wicked and fatal of all sins. It locks Heaven's door and opens the wretched chasms of Hell! Unbelief has slain its millions and damned multitudes. Unbelief drove Adam and Eve from the Edenic Garden and plunged multitudes beneath the judgment waters of the Flood. Unbelief kept Israel out of Canaan for forty years and hindered the fulfillment of God's wondrous promises to His people.

God's Holy Book teaches us that we are saved by believing: "Believe on the Lord Jesus Christ, and thou shalt be saved, and thy house" (Acts 16:31). "That if thou shalt confess with thy mouth the Lord Jesus, and shalt believe in thine heart that God hath raised him from the dead, thou shalt be saved" (Rom. 10:9).

It is impossible to be saved without faith in the glorious Person of Christ. We are saved by believing and damned by not believing! "He that believeth on him is not condemned: but he that believeth not is condemned already, because he hath not believed in the name of the only begotten Son of God" (John 3:18).

God is omnipotent, but one thing He cannot do is to save a lost man or woman who refuses to believe the divine record of His unspeakable Gift! "He did not many mighty works there because of their unbelief" (Matt. 13:58). He cannot perform the mighty

work of regeneration in the human heart until there is the willingness to believe.

Oh, soul without Christ, believe today! Believe that He came
from Heaven by way of a virgin; believe that He walked among
men living a spotless life; believe that He died on the cross, the
just for the unjust; believe that God laid on Him at Calvary all
your sins; believe that He arose from death that ye might have
eternal life! Believe and live!

Satan has his many subtle maneuvers to keep lost men and
women from believing. He has his gospel of "works." He leads
multitudes to believe that church membership and baptism are
efficacious. He causes many to seek "feeling" instead of exer-
cising "faith."

It has been said that, in one of Martin Luther's great conflicts
with the Devil, Satan asked him if he felt his sins were forgiven.
"No," said Martin Luther, "I do not feel that they are forgiven;
but I know they are because God says so in His Word." The Book
of God does not say, "Believe and *feel* saved," but, "Believe and
be saved!"

You can believe that Jesus will receive you if you come to Him.
One of the greatest promises in the Bible is John 6:37, "Him that
cometh to me I will in no wise cast out." Lost soul, look to God
today with hope and confidence. Jesus will save you, cleanse you,
forgive you and make you His forever! He will save the young
and old, the rich and poor, the learned and unlearned. He is no
respecter of persons. Come to Him now.

II. PEOPLE DIE IN SIN BECAUSE OF
PROCRASTINATION

So many times throughout the Bible, God urges the lost to make
great haste in coming to Him. That great chapter 12 of Exodus
deals with the Passover Lamb as typical of God's Lamb. He
expresses the *urgency* of salvation, saying, "Ye shall eat it in
haste: it is the Lord's passover." The people in the bondage and

servitude of Egypt were not to delay. God's provision had been made for their escape and deliverance. "Make haste," God urges, and be saved!

In Isaiah 1:18 He says, "Come now, and let us reason together . . . though your sins be as scarlet, they shall be as white as snow; though they be red like crimson, they shall be as wool." God says, "Come now"—not sometime, not later, but "now."

Perhaps the most subtle trick the Devil has ever used is that of procrastination. While God says, "Today," Satan says, "Tomorrow." Two soul-searching Scriptures should be seriously considered: "Boast not thyself of to morrow; for thou knowest not what a day may bring forth" (Prov. 27:1); "Wherefore (as the Holy Ghost saith, To day if ye will hear his voice, Harden not your hearts . . ." (Heb. 3:7, 8).

Oh, the awful tragedies which have befallen those who have put off salvation!

Recently another Christian man and I went to a man's place of business. We spent two or three hours praying and pleading and explaining the way of salvation. The sinner put it off and delayed because his business was more important to him. He had to make a living. He must work on Sunday to provide for his family, he thought.

In less than a week following our visit, his place of business burned to the ground! God destroyed the thing he thought more important than his soul.

As I stood and looked at the heap of ashes and rubbish, I said to myself, *Oh, the folly of putting off being saved!*

Felix put if off, saying, "Go thy way for this time; when I have a convenient season, I will call for thee." The convenient time never came, and today poor Felix is in Hell.

Agrippa procrastinated, saying, "Almost thou persuadest me to be a Christian." He, too, lost his soul and died in his sins!

Pilate also fell for Satan's subtlety and cried out, "What shall I do then with Jesus which is called Christ?" Without a doubt

Pilate sealed his own doom, cut himself off from God forever and died in his sins.

Men have lost their lives because they waited too long to seek the help of doctors and medical science. Farmers have lost their crops because they delayed sowing and reaping. Merchants have lost their businesses because they waited too long to take inventory and find out where they stood. Men have lost their homes and families while hesitating to live right, to show love and devotion to their wives and children.

Life's greatest blunder, however, is to put off accepting Jesus. This is a mistake beyond repair, a tragedy for which there is no remedy, no solution. This tragedy is fatal, final and irrevocable. May God's blessed Holy Spirit help you to see that salvation is urgent, personal, and demands immediate attention.

III. PEOPLE DIE IN SIN BECAUSE OF SUDDEN DEATH

The Bible speaks clearly about the brevity and uncertainty of life. The ancient preacher Solomon said, "There is no man that hath power over the spirit to retain the spirit; neither hath he power in the day of death..." (Eccles. 8:8). No power on earth, no amount of money or influence, can prolong life one breath longer than the will of God dictates. Man has an appointment with death which he cannot escape. God says, "And as it is appointed unto men once to die, but after this the judgment." How dangerous to defy God, to gamble with eternity!

In years of dealing with unsaved men and women and young people, I have seen many lose their souls. Many whom I have prayed for, wept over, dealt with, have died without Christ and without hope.

In a revival campaign where I preached for two weeks under a big tent, three men died suddenly, their deaths only a few hours apart. One night while preaching I made this statement, "I have never known a great revival, when scores of people are being saved as they are here, but what someone went out to meet God unprepared.'' Little did I know of the sudden death and tragedy which was soon to strike.

The very next morning a fifty-four-year-old man suddenly died of a heart attack in the arms of one of the young men of the church. I had personally dealt with him many times. This businessman was well-to-do and, he thought, self-sufficient. He had promised me more than once that he would be saved and attend church with his family. But he died suddenly, unexpectedly, without warning. I preached his sad funeral.

The day following his death, which occurred within three blocks of the big revival tent, a twenty-nine-year-old man was suddenly killed. He, too, had often been preached to and prayed for. His mother, his sisters and other members of the family were godly people and had often spoken to him of his need. While at work at a large automobile plant, he took one step backwards and fell thirty feet from a scaffold to his death.

With fear and trembling, we preached his funeral. The revival continued, and many were saved.

The day following his sudden death, a forty-year-old man, strong and athletic, died on the operating table in one of the city hospitals. This head football coach at a nearby high school had been to church and had raised his hand for prayer but had put off being saved. His godly brother, a member of the church, had often brought him to the meetings and prayed for his salvation. Now, during a routine operation where no complications were expected, he suddenly died.

''It is appointed unto men once to die'' are God's words. How unwise to take needless risk with your soul! I have known teenagers, young adults and young married people to be taken suddenly. It has always happened thus and always will happen. Nothing is more uncertain than life. No wonder God so often pleads for sinners to come to Him with haste and without delay.

IV. MEN DIE IN SIN BECAUSE THEY GRIEVE AWAY THE HOLY SPIRIT

Many Scriptures teach that God's Holy Spirit can be so grieved and hurt that He no longer pleads and convicts. The familiar passage in Genesis 6:3 bears this out: "My spirit shall not always strive with man." God says there can come a time when His Holy Spirit will no more tolerate unbelief, procrastination and defiance. God sets a deadline! One can only go so far and no further.

This is the age when, in the plan and purpose of God, great emphasis is placed upon the Holy Spirit. Jesus said:

"Nevertheless I tell you the truth; It is expedient for you that I go away: for if I go not away, the Comforter will not come unto you; but if I depart, I will send him unto you. And when he is come, he will reprove the world of sin, and of righteousness, and of judgment...."—John 16:7, 8.

Jesus sent the blessed Holy Spirit to convict of sin. He is in the world testifying of Jesus, speaking to the hearts of the unsaved. He is holy, sensitive and personal and can be grieved away by constant rejection. The Holy Spirit will not always strive with rebellious and incorrigible hearts.

He ceased to strive with Pharaoh as He pled with him, saying, "How long wilt thou refuse to humble thyself before me?" (Exod. 10:3). We read ten times in Exodus of the solemn fact that "the Lord hardened Pharaoh's heart...." Finally, God's preacher, Moses, said, "I will see thy face again no more" (Exod. 10:29). Think of it! No more will God's man pray, preach, weep— "no more." God has finished with Pharaoh. He will die in sin!

The Bible records others whom God forsook and spoke to no more, allowing them to die in sin. Yes, Pharaoh, Nabal, wicked Herod, Felix, Agrippa and many others are set forth in the divine record as living examples of the awful truth, "My spirit shall not always strive with man."

God told Jeremiah three times not to pray for the wicked people of Jerusalem: "Therefore pray not thou for this people, neither lift up cry nor prayer for them, neither make intercession to me: for I will not hear thee."

Oh, fatal moment for your precious soul when prayers and tears can no longer avail!

It is possible for an unsaved person to be "past feeling." The Lord Jesus Christ can save from adultery, murder and profanity; but when the Holy Spirit no longer speaks and the Father no longer listens to loved ones when they pray for you, then you have crossed God's deadline. Be not deceived: God's patience does wear out; for three times in Romans, chapter 1, is this awful expression, "God gave them up."

History records a solemn moment in the career of the great Napoleon Bonaparte. In the midst of a smoking battlefield, one of his soldiers came running to him, crying out, "We have won! We have won!" It is said that as the great military genius looked out over the battlefields and saw many of his soldiers wounded and dead, he said, "One other such victory will cost me my kingdom."

You may turn down Jesus and refuse His mercy and grace. You may feel you are winning the victory over the prayers, tears and tender efforts of God's people to get you saved. But one day such a seeming victory will cost you your soul.

V. MEN DIE IN SIN BECAUSE OF THE WORK OF SATAN

Satan's master plan is to send you to Hell, so he uses all his satanic cunning and wisdom to keep you from repenting and believing and being saved. He fought to keep the Saviour from coming into the world; he has concocted "another gospel" and organized his "ministers of righteousness." He has schemed, deceived and blinded the eyes of millions to the truth of the Gospel of grace. From the moment God drove him from the Garden of Eden until now, Satan has been active night and day. No wonder the Bible warns us, "Be sober, be vigilant; because your adversary the devil, as a roaring lion, walketh about, seeking whom he may devour" (I Pet. 5:8).

We must admit that Satan has the power to blind the unsaved, to keep them in the dark, to hinder them from being saved. Paul said:

"But if our gospel be hid, it is hid to them that are lost: In whom the god of this world hath blinded the minds of them which believe not, lest the light of the glorious gospel of Christ, who is the image of God, should shine unto them."—II Cor. 4:3, 4.

Satan had deceived these people to whom Jesus said, "Ye... shall die in your sins: whither I go, ye cannot come." Jesus told them:

"Ye are of your father the devil, and the lusts of your father ye will do. He was a murderer from the beginning, and abode not in the truth, because there is no truth in him. When he speaketh a lie, he speaketh of his own: for he is a liar, and the father of it."—John 8:44.

It is difficult to see why an intelligent human being would want to stay one of the Devil's children. He is a poor provider; you cannot depend on his word; he is not to be trusted. His poison is sugar-coated, and all his pleasures are "just for a season." He cannot comfort you when your heart is broken. He has never dried a tear nor lifted a heavy burden. He offers no hope in death, no help for the life to come. In fact, his own doom is sealed. God will put him in the "lake of fire" one day, along with all those who are deceived by him. "And the devil that deceived them was cast into the lake of fire and brimstone, where the beast and the false prophet are, and shall be tormented day and night for ever and ever" (Rev. 20:10).

When I was a boy, I had some very erroneous ideas about the Devil and Hell. I had seen pictures of Satan with fiery nostrils and hideous face, carrying a pitchfork in his hand. I grew up thinking that he was the king of Hell and would reign over the dark domains of the lost.

Neither of these pictures is true. He is beautiful and refined. He is full of wisdom, and all his schemes sound good. He will not reign in Hell but will be tormented forever with all sinners.

As one of God's preachers, may I beg you to turn your back on the Devil. Do not be misled or deceived by him any longer. To follow him, to listen to him, to be deceived by him mean to be forever lost.

Jesus speaks of two great things in this text: namely, death and Heaven. When He said, "Ye shall die in your sins," He spoke of death. When He said, "Whither I go, ye cannot come," He spoke of Heaven. How wonderful to die in peace and with the hope of Heaven. To die as a Christian means to "die in the Lord" and "to be absent from the body, and present with the Lord."

The poor thief on the cross, who had lived all his life in sin, turned to Jesus before he died and was wonderfully saved. Jesus said to him, "To day shalt thou be with me in paradise." You need not die in your sins; you can be saved. He loves you, wants you, welcomes you.

I have preached thousands of sermons in my years of ministry; but very few times have I preached without quoting John 6:37, "All that the Father giveth me shall come to me; and him that cometh to me I will in no wise cast out." Come to Jesus; He will take you as you are. He loves you and cares for your soul as much as He has ever loved or cared for any individual in history. He reaches out His hand to you. Oh, come to Him now!

One of the sweetest little stories I have ever heard was one which concerned a little seven-year-old girl who had strayed out of the house and into a beautiful flower garden nearby where a great man of God was praying and meditating. When the mother found her little daughter, she was walking up and down the garden hand in hand with the great preacher who was quoting Scripture and talking with the Lord.

Her mother, embarrassed for fear the child had disturbed the servant of God, said, "Come into the house at once. You have interrupted the preacher."

As the mother scolded her, the little child responded, "But, Mama, he reached out his hand to me."

How wonderful that Jesus reaches out His nail-scarred hand to you! God says in His Word, "All day long I have stretched forth my hands unto a disobedient and gainsaying people" (Rom. 10:21). By faith, place your trust in Him and be saved today.

"Ye...shall die in your sins: whither I go, ye cannot come."

Chapter II

Destined for Divine Destruction

First Prize Winner in Sword Evangelistic Sermon Contest, 1959

"A prudent man foreseeth the evil, and hideth himself: but the simple pass on, and are punished."—Prov. 22:3.

Throughout the Word of God great distinction is made between the wise and the foolish. The wise will obey God's Word, while the foolish stumble on in disobedience. "The wise in heart will receive commandments: but a prating fool shall fall" (Prov. 10:8). The wise will be able to understand God's truth, while it is divinely hid from the wicked. "Many shall be purified, and made white, and tried; but the wicked shall do wickedly: and none of the wicked shall understand; but the wise shall understand" (Dan. 12:10).

Jesus also made great distinction between the wise and the foolish. He likened the man who would hear and obey His Gospel to a wise builder whose house, built upon a rock, would stand all the fierce storms of life. He likened the man who hears the Word of God and refuses to believe to a foolish man who built his house upon the sinking sands of this wicked world. Here are His words:

"Therefore whosoever heareth these sayings of mine, and doeth them, I will liken him unto a wise man, which built his house upon a rock: And the rain descended, and the floods came, and the winds

blew, and beat upon that house; and it fell not: for it was founded upon a rock. And every one that heareth these sayings of mine, and doeth them not, shall be likened unto a foolish man, which built his house upon the sand: And the rain descended, and the floods came, and the winds blew, and beat upon that house; and it fell: and great was the fall of it.''—Matt. 7:24-27.

In Matthew 25 Jesus also spoke of the wise and foolish virgins— the wise being saved and ready for the second coming of Christ, while the foolish remain religious but lost until the door of mercy closes forever.

''Then shall the kingdom of heaven be likened unto ten virgins, which took their lamps, and went forth to meet the bridegroom. And five of them were wise, and five were foolish. They that were foolish took lamps, and took no oil with them: But the wise took oil in their vessels with their lamps. While the bridegroom tarried, they all slumbered and slept. And at midnight there was a cry made, Behold, the bridegroom cometh; go ye out to meet him. Then all those virgins arose, and trimmed their lamps. And the foolish said unto the wise, Give us of your oil; for our lamps are gone out. But the wise answered, saying, Not so; lest there be not enough for us and you: but go ye rather to them that sell, and buy for yourselves. And while they went to buy, the bridegroom came; and they that were ready went in with him to the marriage: and the door was shut. Afterward came also the other virgins, saying, Lord, Lord, open to us. But he answered and said, Verily I say unto you, I know you not. Watch therefore, for ye know neither the day nor the hour wherein the Son of man cometh.''—Vss. 1-13.

Those who are wise in the eyes of God emphasize the spiritual; the foolish, the carnal. The wise emphasize the eternal, while the foolish live only for the temporal. The wise man gives pre-eminence to the soul; the foolish gives the emphasis to the body. The wise give emphasis to the unseen, while the foolish live only for that which they can see. The wise live for the world to come, while the foolish follow the philosophy, "Eat, drink, and be merry," and live only for the world of today.

To put the matter into language easily understood by all: the Bible teaches that the man or woman who gets saved from sin is acting the part of wisdom. The one, however, who procrastinates and takes lightly the matter of his soul's destiny is playing the part of a fool.

Solomon, perhaps the wisest man who ever lived, said, "A prudent [wise] man foreseeth the evil, and hideth himself: but the simple [foolish] pass on, and are punished."

I. THEY PASS ON IN SPITE OF
REPEATED WARNINGS

We are commanded to warn the lost of the penalty of sin, the day of judgment and the wrath of God.

"When I say unto the wicked, O wicked man, thou shalt surely die; if thou dost not speak to warn the wicked from his way, that wicked man shall die in his iniquity; but his blood will I require at thine hand."—Ezek. 33:8.

Those who die in their sins do not go to Hell without warning.

Wicked Pharaoh was not without warning, for God said to him, "How long wilt thou refuse to humble thyself before me?"

Pleasure-mad Belshazzar was not without warning, for he had seen how God had humbled proud Nebuchadnezzar, his grandfather. Before God weighed Belshazzar in the divine balances and found him wanting, he had been warned by the preaching, prophecy and godly life of the Prophet Daniel.

Pilate, the fence-straddling, pussyfooting politician, did not go to Hell without warning; for his wife sent him a most timely note which read, "Have thou nothing to do with that just man: for I have suffered many things this day in a dream because of him" (Matt. 27:19). As Pilate stood at the crossroads of all eternity, about to decide between Christ and a murderer, Heaven or Hell, the solemn warning came; but since it went unheeded, Pilate is now in Hell.

The rich fool of Luke was not without warning. Doubtlessly he had heard of the parables, sermons and miracles of Jesus; but engrossed in his wealth and blind to his needs, he died without hope. God said, "...this night thy soul shall be required of thee: then whose shall those things be, which thou hast provided?"

In many years of preaching and witnessing, I have seen scores, over the warnings of God, pass on and lose their souls.

I visited a most brokenhearted man in the hospital. His young wife and two little children had burned to death in their home. He was so pitifully burned trying to effect a rescue that he could not even attend their funeral. As I sat at his bedside, he said, "I used to come to hear you preach; I am lost, and I have no one to blame but myself." His wife was not without warning. Some of our workers had pled with her to be saved less than a week before.

A fifty-four-year-old woman, recently killed suddenly by a car in my city, was repeatedly witnessed to and prayed with by several godly people of my acquaintance. She passed on over God's solemn warning and lost her soul.

II. THEY PASS ON OVER THE WOOING OF THE HOLY SPIRIT

Scriptures teach that the Holy Spirit speaks to the hearts of men. Just as "the Spirit of God moved upon the face of the waters" in transforming, recreative power, so He moves upon the lives of men to bring them to Christ. In John 16 Jesus clearly taught that the Holy Spirit would come to convict men of sin!

"Nevertheless I tell you the truth; It is expedient for you that I go away: for if I go not away, the Comforter will not come unto you; but if I depart, I will send him unto you. And when he is come, he will reprove the world of sin, and of righteousness, and of

judgment: Of sin, because they believe not on me; Of righteous-
ness, because I go to my Father, and ye see me no more; Of judg-
ment, because the prince of this world is judged."—Vss. 7-11.

He is in the world to reprove and convict the unsaved. His con-
victing work is not to be trifled with, nor to be ignored, because
God says, "My spirit shall not always strive with man."

The wonderful work of the Holy Spirit can be spurned, ignored,
rejected and denied. In fact, it is possible to oppose His work so
that He will go away, never to speak to that heart again. Jesus
spoke of a most weighty matter when He warned against the
blasphemy against the Holy Spirit or speaking against Him:

"Wherefore I say unto you, All manner of sin and blasphemy
shall be forgiven unto men: but the blasphemy against the Holy
Ghost shall not be forgiven unto men. And whosoever speaketh
a word against the Son of man, it shall be forgiven him: but
whosoever speaketh against the Holy Ghost, it shall not be for-
given him, neither in this world, neither in the world to come."—
Matt. 12:31, 32.

I think it possible for many to cross God's divine deadline.
Remember that this is the age of the Holy Spirit—from the day
of Pentecost until the coming of Christ. In a dispensation where
God's Word gives great emphasis to the Holy Spirit, it is reason-
able to believe that He deals with many; and many can sin against
Him.

A lady came forward with others to accept Christ as her personal Saviour, and she was gloriously transformed by the power
of the Holy Spirit. After the service was over and tears of joy
were still on her face, she said, "Brother Tom, I would like to
ask you a question. I heard you tell today how God had laid all
of my sin upon Jesus and that Jesus had completely satisfied the
justice of God for me. When the invitation song was being sung,
I had such a strange experience: I felt as if something were literally pulling me to leave my seat and come to accept Christ

publicly. Now what I want to know is this: What was that strange power pulling at me?''

I said, "Lady, it was not some*thing*; it was Some*one*—the Holy Spirit of God!''

He speaks to men; He mourns over them and broods over them; He brings pressure to bear to get them saved. Oh, the folly of resisting His conviction!

You may say, "Preacher, I'll never go that far. I'll never turn Him away forever." Remember, however, the crossing of God's deadline may be a gradual process; and you may be in the midst of that process.

It seems there may be about five steps which could lead one across the deadline and too far down the stream of unbelief ever to turn back. These five steps are:

1. Resisting the strivings of the Holy Spirit. "My spirit shall not always strive with man" (Gen. 6:3).

2. Refusing to humble yourself before God. "How long wilt thou refuse to humble thyself before me?" (Exod. 10:3).

3. Refusing to be drawn to Christ. "No man can come to me, except the Father which hath sent me draw him" (John 6:44).

4. Neglecting God's salvation. "How shall we escape, if we neglect so great salvation?" (Heb. 2:3).

5. Hardening your heart against the voice of God. "Wherefore (as the Holy Ghost saith, To day if ye will hear his voice, Harden not your hearts, as in the provocation..." (Heb. 3:7, 8).

Some years ago I was speaking one morning on the radio on resisting the Holy Spirit and going on in sin until the patience of God wears out.

I left the studio and drove to my office. Just as I drove up in front of the office, an old man drove up also and stopped his car. His hair was as white as snow; he had already lived his three-score years and ten. When he rolled down the window, I could see tears course down his wrinkled face. He said, "Preacher, I just finished listening to you. My heart is gripped with the awful fear that I might have gone too far. Can you tell me—is there any hope for an old sinner like me? Have I waited too long?"

I said to him, "My friend, your broken heart, your tear-stained face, your anxious inquiry—all tell me that you have not gone too far, that you can be saved."

He was saved and lived a few more years. He read the Bible and prayed and witnessed to others. He died and went to Heaven.

If you feel that God is speaking to you today, thank God for it and make the most of it. For the sake of your soul, do not resist the voice of the Holy Spirit; but yield to His pressure even now and by faith accept Christ as your Saviour and Friend.

III. THEY PASS ON OVER THE WEEPING OF GOD'S PEOPLE

Once when David was in hiding from Saul and was in great distress and frustration, he said, "I looked on my right hand, and beheld, but there was no man that would know me: refuge failed me; no man cared for my soul" (Ps. 142:4). David actually felt that no one cared for his soul, but such was not the case. Jonathan was one who loved him dearly and risked his life for him.

It is very doubtful that you could say no one cares for your soul. Someone loves you, prays for you and weeps over your lost condition.

Moses was greatly distressed over the sins of his people. They had grievously sinned in breaking God's law and worshiping the false god. Moses prayed, "Yet now, if thou wilt forgive their sin—; and if not, blot me, I pray thee, out of thy book which thou hast written" (Exod. 32:32). Not one Israelite could ever say, "No man cares for my soul or prays for me."

The Apostle Paul prayed for his lost relatives and friends. He cared:

"I say the truth in Christ, I lie not, my conscience also bearing

me witness in the Holy Ghost, That I have great heaviness and continual sorrow in my heart. For I could wish that myself were accursed from Christ for my brethren, my kinsmen according to the flesh. "—Rom. 9:1-3.

"Brethren, my heart's desire and prayer to God for Israel is, that they might be saved. "—Rom. 10:1.

I have seen hundreds of Christians weep over their lost loved ones. I have heard the father in a family sob from a broken heart, "O God, save my son!" I have heard gray-haired mothers pray for their children until my own heart was melted. How often I have seen wives weep and heard them pray for their husbands to be saved.

Some time ago while conducting a revival campaign, a fine young man told me his father would be in the service the next night and asked me to pray for him.

The next night his dad came and heard the Gospel. While others were coming to be saved, the son went to his father's side, put his arms about him, wept aloud and begged him to be saved. The dad did not come forward that night, but he came at a later service.

As I went from the church that night, I thought, *If he doesn't get saved, I wouldn't want to stand in that dad's shoes on judgment day.*

God sees the tears of His people, as He saw David's, and He never forgets: "Thou tellest my wanderings: put thou my tears into thy bottle: are they not in thy book?" (Ps. 56:8). Surely Jesus must weep over sinners, too, for He loves them so. He once "beheld the city [Jerusalem], and wept over it."

Oh, t he folly of walking over the tears of a sainted loved one!

One night a Christian woman came to me at the beginning of the service and said, "Pray for my husband; he is lost and is here tonight."

I preached, and several came to be saved but not the lost husband. After the service, I went to talk to him. During our conver-

sation, he made the statement that he didn't believe there was a
Hell just because Jesus said so.

His fourteen-year-old son, with his Bible under his arm, had
stepped up beside his dad. He listened to all that was said. When
the lost man said, "I don't believe there is a Hell just because
Jesus said so," his young son cried aloud, "O Daddy, Daddy!
Don't call Jesus a liar! We love you, Daddy, and so does Jesus!
Please believe Him. He would not lie to you."

I thought again, *I would not for all the money in the world stand
in that man's shoes when God settles the score on judgment day.*

Oh, the folly of passing on over the tears, the prayers, the plead-
ings, the broken heart, the faithful love and devotion of those to
whom your soul is precious!

IV. THEY PASS ON IN SPITE OF
THE CROSS OF CHRIST

"For the preaching of the cross is to them that perish foolishness; but unto us which are saved it is the power of God." Like
the two thieves who were crucified on Calvary on either side of
Christ, you are on the right or the wrong side of the cross. On
the one hand, a man died in rejection and unbelief; while on the
other side, a man died in faith and went immediately into Paradise with Jesus.

The word *cross* is found no less than twenty-eight times in the
New Testament. It is also seen in the Old Testament in types and
symbols.

I see the cross in Abel's lamb whose blood was sprinkled on
the altar.

I see the cross in the ark as judgment falls upon it.

I see the cross in the passover lamb as the basis for God's forgiveness and deliverance.

I see the cross in the rock smitten by Moses, for the Bible says
that it "pleased God to bruise him."

I see the cross in the brazen serpent lifted up so dying people could look and live.

In Paul's writings we find "the death of the cross" (Phil. 2:8); "the blood of the cross" (Col.1:20); "the offense of the cross" (Gal. 5:11); the glory of the cross (Gal. 6:14); "the preaching of the cross" (I Cor. 1:18).

The cross cannot be ignored! It must be reckoned with. It is God's altar where, in the death of His own Son, He perfected redemption for all who trust Him. It is the moral axis of all God's universe around which the wheels of redemption move.

The cross of Christ sweeps away all of man's pretense of being good; it removes all pretense of being saved by works.

"All we like sheep have gone astray; we have turned every one to his own way; and the Lord hath laid on him the iniquity of us all." This is the only verse in the Bible which begins and ends with the word *all.* One *all* shows all have sinned; the other shows that "all" our iniquity was laid upon Him.

Thank God for the old rugged cross, stained with divine and royal blood! The cross of Jesus shows man at his worst and God's grace at its best. It reveals God's grace and love and shows man's sin and rebellion. It shows the depths of man's ruin and the height of God's redemption. See that cross on the skull-shaped hill of Calvary, and hear God's soul-searching inquiry, "Is it nothing to you, all ye that pass by?"

You must take your stand on one side of Calvary or the other. "But God forbid that I should glory, save in the cross of our Lord Jesus Christ, by whom the world is crucified unto me, and I unto the world" (Gal. 6:14).

The cross means much to God; it is the theme of all Heaven's music, the power of all gospel preaching, the only hope of a lost world, and the only safe refuge from God's wrath and judgment. No wonder an ancient writer penned these lines:

What Thou, my Lord, hast suffered
Was all for sinners' gain;

> Mine, mine was the transgression,
>   But Thine the deadly pain.
> Lo, here I fall, my Saviour,
>   'Tis I deserve Thy place;
> Look on me with Thy favor;
>   Vouchsafe to me Thy grace.
>
> What language shall I borrow
>   To thank Thee, dearest Friend,
> For this, Thy dying sorrow,
>   Thy pity without end?
> Oh, make me Thine forever;
>   And should I fainting be,
> Lord, let me never, never
>   Outlive my love to Thee.

V. THEY PASS ON IN SPITE OF GOD'S LOVE

Oh, love of God! What tongue can explain Thee? Thou lovest sinners without a reason. "Herein is love, not that we loved God, but that he loved us, and sent his Son to be the propitiation for our sins" (I John 4:10).

Thou lovest without limitation: "For God so loved the world, that he gave his only begotten Son, that whosoever believeth in him should not perish, but have everlasting life" (John 3:16).

Thou lovest without end: "The LORD hath appeared of old unto me, saying, Yea, I have loved thee with an everlasting love: therefore with lovingkindness have I drawn thee" (Jer. 31:3).

In the Scriptures, God's love is likened unto three earthly loves:

1. A father's pity (Ps. 103:13);
2. A mother's love (Isa. 49:15);
3. A bridegroom's affection (Eph. 5:25).

The Saviour who loves with such infinite love knocks at your heart's door today. "Behold, I stand at the door, and knock: if any man hear my voice, and open the door, I will come in to him, and will sup with him, and he with me." He has knocked often. He knocks sometimes quietly, sometimes loudly. Someday the last knock will come, but He stands now on the outside knocking, begging, pleading to come in.

The newspapers some years ago carried a most sympathetic article concerning a Dr. Lorenz, a famous physician and surgeon of Vienna, in Austria. People from all over the world sought the healing touch of this famous physician who had seemingly cured some incurables.

One afternoon the papers told how a mother and her little crippled girl, sitting in their home on a rainy afternoon, were talking about the girl's affliction. The child said, "Mother, wouldn't it be wonderful if I could get an appointment with this famous physician? He could straighten my crippled and crooked limbs."

The mother said, "But, dear, it would cost thousands of dollars. And many people, with much money, have sought his services but to no avail. You could never get to him."

At that very moment, unbeknown to the girl and her mother, Dr. Lorenz had stepped out on the street in that very city to take a little walk for some fresh air and exercise. When it began to rain, he turned aside and stepped up on the porch of this very home and knocked on the door. He was a stranger to this mother and her crippled child. He asked, "May I come in? I would like to call for my carriage."

The mother, seeing only a stranger, said, "No. We admit no strangers to our home. Make your call elsewhere."

When the newspaper the next day carried the story that the famous Dr. Lorenz had been refused admittance into a humble home in that city, the little girl cried out, "Mother! Mother! He was here! I needed him so much, but we wouldn't let him in!"

Friend, you need Christ. He is knocking at your heart's door. He knocks through the sermon. He knocks through the invitation hymn. He knocks through the prayers of the people of God, your Christian friends and loved ones. He knocks through a gospel tract. He knocks through the changed life of every Christian you have ever observed. He knocks through the Holy Spirit. You are the only one who can open the door. That door must always be opened from the inside. Jesus never opens it against your will. Hear Him knocking. Hear Him pleading. See Him standing outside. May God help you to let Him come in today and save your soul.

"A prudent man foreseeth the evil, and hideth himself: but the simple pass on, and are punished."—Prov. 22:3.

Chapter III

When Rags and Riches Walk Together

First Prize Winner in Sword Evangelistic Sermon Contest, 1957

"The rich and poor meet together: the Lord is the maker of them all."—Prov. 22:2.

The rich and the poor have more in common than this world ever dreamed of. In the eyes of men, they may seem to live in two different worlds. From the world's view, they may seem to be as far apart as the two poles; but in the eyes of Almighty God, they have much in common. They "meet together" on many points.

Jesus often talked of "the rich and poor" in the same conversation. He spoke of "the rich and poor" together in the familiar 16th chapter of Luke:

"There was a certain rich man, which was clothed in purple and fine linen, and fared sumptuously every day: And there was a certain beggar named Lazarus, which was laid at his gate, full of sores, And desiring to be fed with the crumbs which fell from the rich man's table: moreover the dogs came and licked his sores. And it came to pass, that the beggar died, and was carried by the angels into Abraham's bosom: the rich man also died, and was buried; And in hell he lift up his eyes, being in torments, and

seeth Abraham afar off, and Lazarus in his bosom.''—Vss. 19-23.

This is the tragic account of a rich man who lost his soul and at this moment suffers the anguish, torment and remorse of the lost in Hell. The poor man died and went to Abraham's bosom (Heaven before the resurrection of Jesus) and at this moment is in the presence of God and of angels.

The rich man was not lost because of his wealth, nor was the poor beggar saved because of his poverty. The rich man went to Hell because he rejected Christ, and the poor man was saved because of his personal faith in the Son of God.

Jesus also spoke of the rich and the poor when He sat in the temple in Jerusalem and saw the poor come to cast in their gifts into the treasury.

"And he looked up, and saw the rich men casting their gifts into the treasury. And he saw also a certain poor widow casting in thither two mites. And he said, Of a truth I say unto you, that this poor widow hath cast in more than they all: For all these have of their abundance cast in unto the offerings of God: but she of her penury hath cast in all the living that she had.''—Luke 21:1-4.

Here we see that Jesus watched the "rich and poor meet together," and He weighed with divine wisdom and scrutiny their actions, and a record was made in the books of Heaven. The onlookers that day probably applauded the gifts of the rich and looked with disdain upon the widow's mite; but in the records on High and in the mind of the Judge of all the earth, the poor widow had made an eternal impression, while the gifts of the rich brought no commendation from our Lord.

My friends, how important it is to try to see things as God sees them!

There are so many wonderful and precious things which money will not buy. No rich man with his money ever bought peace of heart and mind or forgiveness of sins or a home in Heaven. Money cannot buy the love and loyalty of a good and faithful wife nor the honor and joy which is afforded by godly Christian children nor the happiness of a real Christian home where Jesus is the silent Listener to every conversation and the unseen Guest at every meal! Money cannot quiet the cries of a guilty conscience nor heal the bloody wounds of a wasted life.

Be not fooled by the deceitfulness of riches nor blinded by the treachery of sinful pleasures. Money cannot buy a good name nor the respect and admiration of one's associates. The wise man said, "A good name is rather to be chosen than great riches, and loving favour than silver and gold. The rich and poor meet together: the Lord is the maker of them all" (Prov. 22:1, 2).

I. THEY MEET TOGETHER IN DEATH

Hebrews 9:27 says, ". . . it is appointed unto men [all men] once to die, but after this the judgment."

And we read in James 1:9-11:

"Let the brother of low degree rejoice in that he is exalted: But the rich, in that he is made low: because as the flower of the grass he shall pass away. For the sun is no sooner risen with a burning heat, but it withereth the grass, and the flower thereof falleth, and the grace of the fashion of it perisheth: so also shall the rich man fade away in his ways."

When God's appointed hour comes for men to die, all of the riches of earth cannot buy another heartbeat nor one more breath of air.

I recently read of a soul-winning preacher who went to see a businessman about his soul. The following conversation took place:

"What is your business here?" asked the businessman.

"I came to speak to you about your soul, but I see you are very busy."

"Yes, I am very busy," said the most disinterested man of wealth.

The man of God put out his hand to say good-by and, drawing close to the astonished man, whispered solemnly in his ear, "Suppose I had been Death."

Men must look ahead and prepare for the inevitable hour of death. They must 'number their days and apply their hearts to wisdom.'

God's Book gives great emphasis to the brevity of human life. It is as a shadow passing quickly across the face of the earth; it is as a vapor, fragile and unstable and soon gone; it is as grass, green a moment, then dry and dead! Yes, as the Bible says, man's life "appeareth for a little time, and then vanisheth away."

Death is no respecter of persons. Death never stops to consider whether one be rich or poor, whether one lives in a palace of luxury or a little hut of poverty. Death comes uninvited, suddenly, unexpected! In forty-five years I have seen hundreds on their deathbeds. I have heard them sing the songs of Zion as they loosed the cords of earthly life and became "absent from the body, and...present with the Lord." I have also seen them die with a curse upon their lips and a heart full of hatred toward God and go out into the darkness of Hell.

I have been at the bedside of the wealthy as well as that of the poor. And I declare unto you that neither riches nor poverty means very much in that most solemn moment when a man goes out to meet the God who made him and the Saviour who died for him.

Some years ago I read the sermon of an old-time preacher who told a story which, as I remember, went something like this:

The lovely daughter of a most wealthy man lay dying and was soon to meet God. It is said that the wealthy man called the doctor outside the sick room and said, "Now listen, Doctor. Money is no problem. As you know, I am a wealthy man. If you can save my daughter from death and make her well, I will make you rich. You name your price, and I'll meet it."

The doctor replied, "Sir, I am just a physician. I can neither give life, nor have I the right to take it. If I could heal your lovely daughter, I would; but, Sir, I am not God; you had better be talking to Him."

II. THEY MEET TOGETHER IN SORROW

All people have sorrow and tears, and the road of life is paved with heartaches and burdens. What erroneous thinking it is that the poor have all the sorrow and the rich have none! Trouble and sorrow are no respecters of persons.

Job says, "Yet man is born unto trouble, as the sparks fly upward" (5:7). He also wisely said, "Man [all men] that is born of a woman is of few days, and full of trouble" (14:1).

Riches do not fortify the wealthy against sorrow and tears; in fact, the Bible plainly teaches that so often riches cause trouble and heartache.

"But godliness with contentment is great gain. For we brought nothing into this world, and it is certain we can carry nothing out. And having food and raiment let us be therewith content. But they that will be rich fall into temptation and a snare, and into many foolish and hurtful lusts, which drown men in destruction and perdition. For the love of money is the root of all evil: which while some coveted after, they have erred from the faith, and pierced themselves through with many sorrows."—I Tim. 6:6-10.

Some years ago a fine-looking, middle-aged woman drove up in a large and beautiful car in front of our home. She came to our door and asked for a few minutes of our time. As my wife and I listened, she told this story from a broken heart and with many tears:

When I was a young girl, I made a profession of being a Christian; but it was not real, I'm sure, for I have lived everything but a Christian life. I married an unsaved man, and we have lived without God, and we have no hope.

My husband is the vice-president of a large company (she

named a large dairy product company). We belong to the Country Club; we are rich in this world's goods. Our personal friends are wealthy too; but I am in trouble. My only son is in jail; he has committed an awful sin and awaits his sentence to prison. My husband and I are in shame and disgrace. We have not slept for nights.

Then she held up her hands toward Mrs. Malone, and upon her fingers were thousands of dollars' worth of diamonds. Her face was wet with tears as she said,

I would gladly give these jewels and that car you can see through the window and that large palatial home in which we live, if I could go back across the years and be a Christian mother and raise my boy in a godly home.

In a moment she left without giving her name and without letting us say more. As she went sobbing out the door, she cried,

Pray for me. Pray for me. Oh, God, I wish it could be different.

When the troubles of life come, the riches of earth can bring no comfort. Only the presence of Jesus can fortify the soul against the hours of darkness and travail. Remember that, though the sun shines brightly in your little world today and all seems well, trouble and sorrow and tears lie ahead.

III. THEY MEET TOGETHER IN HELL

Jesus constantly warned men that the love of riches could damn their souls. We read in Matthew 19 the tragic record of one young man who came running to Jesus but nevertheless lost his soul because of his unwillingness to repent, believe, and be saved. "But when the young man heard that saying, he went away sorrowful: for he had great possessions."

In Luke 12, Jesus told of another rich man who lost his soul.

"And he spake a parable unto them, saying, The ground of a certain rich man brought forth plentifully: And he thought within himself, saying, What shall I do, because I have no room where to bestow my fruits? And he said, This will I do: I will pull down my barns, and build greater; and there will I bestow all my fruits and my goods. And I will say to my soul, Soul, thou hast much goods laid up for many years; take thine ease, eat, drink and be merry. But God said unto him, Thou fool, this night thy soul shall be required of thee: then whose shall those things be, which thou hast provided?"—Vss. 16–20.

As previously mentioned, Jesus also told in Luke, chapter 16, of a rich man who died in sin and went to Hell. The broad road that leads to Hell is traveled by "many" from all walks of life.

When calling on unsaved people with a pastor in Barberton, Ohio, where I was engaged in a revival campaign, he said to me, "I would like to take a few minutes, Brother Tom, and show you something most interesting."

We drove through a section of the city with some of the most beautiful and spacious buildings, many unoccupied. These buildings were built almost like the great castles of olden days. The preacher told me this story about these buildings.

Some years ago a very wealthy industrialist in the city began to spend his wealth in erecting these beautiful edifices. Friends advised him repeatedly to examine his books and, before going further, stop and consider his financial state. But he refused. But one day when he did weigh his assets against his liabilities, he discovered he was broke and heavily in debt. In a few years he died as a pauper, owing thousands of dollars. He would not listen to good advice. He would not balance his books. He refused to look ahead!

My friend, where are you in the sight of God today—saved or lost? Heaven or Hell—which shall it be?

In Hell the rich and poor alike who have rejected Christ shall bewail forever the wasted life and lament ten million times the lost opportunities to be saved.

Recently I stood at the door of a small and humble home where a very poor family lived. The mother came to the door. I said to her, "I am a preacher, and I came to talk to you about your soul. I want very much to see you saved."

She said to me, "Brother Malone, I am a poor woman. I have had no luxuries of life. I have six children. I have known much illness and trouble. My husband is a drunkard, and my home is like Hell! I think I am living in my hell here on earth, and surely God won't let me suffer in Hell for all eternity."

Poor lost soul! She thought because of sorrow and trouble here God owed her a home in Heaven.

The rich and poor go to Hell who will not accept the kind invitation to come unto Jesus and have life everlasting. "The rich and poor meet together: the Lord is the maker of them all."

IV. THEY MEET TOGETHER IN JUDGMENT

Rich and poor alike shall stand before God in the day of judgment. When the heavens roll up like a scroll and the mountains and islands of earth are moved out of their places, all the unsaved, rich or poor, shall flee from the face of the living Son of God!

"And the kings of the earth, and the great men, and the rich men, and the chief captains, and the mighty men, and every bondman, and every free man, hid themselves in the dens and in the rocks of the mountains; And said to the mountains and rocks, Fall on us, and hide us from the face of him that sitteth on the throne, and from the wrath of the Lamb: For the great day of his wrath is come; and who shall be able to stand?"—Rev. 6:15-17.

The rich and poor alike shall be tormented and made to worship the Antichrist in the Tribulation time after the church has been removed from this earthly scene.

"And he [the Antichrist] *causeth all, both small and great, rich*

*and poor, free and bond, to receive a mark in their right hand,
or in their foreheads: And that no man might buy or sell, save
he that had the mark, or the name of the beast, or the number
of his name.''*—Rev. 13:16, 17.

*"And I saw the dead, small and great, stand before God; and
the books were opened: and another book was opened, which is
the book of life: and the dead were judged out of those things which
were written in the books, according to their works....And
whosoever was not found written in the book of life was cast into
the lake of fire.''*—Rev. 20:12, 15.

When the day of judgment comes and the rich and poor stand
before the Son of God whom they rejected, no man will be asked
whether he was rich or poor. Houses, lands, automobiles and
clothes will long since have become of no importance when that
day of reckoning comes.

Some time ago on a street of our city, I saw two young men
handcuffed together, being taken by a policeman from the courtroom back to the jail. One was clad in the garments of a beggar;
the other was well-dressed and clean. His very appearance spoke
of culture and wealth. But both, I learned, were guilty of the same
offense; both stood before the same judge; both received the same
sentence; and both were to be sent to the same prison.

*"The rich and poor meet together: the Lord is the maker of them
all."*

V. THEY MEET TOGETHER IN SALVATION

Thank God, the Bible teaches that both rich and poor can be
saved. "Abram was very rich in cattle, in silver, and in gold."
Abraham, the friend of God, will be in Heaven. Joseph of
Arimathaea was evidently very rich but loved the Lord Jesus and
begged His body after His crucifixion that he might give Him a
decent burial, thus fulfilling the prophetic statement of Isaiah,

"And he made his grave...with the rich in his death."

The poor beggar who lay starving at the gates of the wicked rich man will be with the rich in Heaven.

The rich and poor met together forty-five years ago in a little country church when I, a lost sinner, met the King of kings and the Lord of lords; and we have been fellowshiping together ever since! The One who owns the earth and the fullness thereof is a Friend of sinners. He who walked home with wealthy Zacchaeus also ate on the hillsides with humble fishermen and drank at the same well with a lost, dissolute woman whom He saved.

"For ye know the grace of our Lord Jesus Christ, that, though he was rich, yet for your sakes he became poor, that ye through his poverty might be rich."—II Cor. 8:9.

I am living with a King! His riches are mine! 'The rich and the poor have met together!'

Some years ago while still a student in college, I was holding a revival meeting in a country church in North Alabama. One afternoon I said to the pastor, "Brother Gardener, I am going to preach tonight on 'The Precious Blood of Jesus.' Can you give me a good true story to illustrate what the blood of Jesus can do for a lost sinner?"

He thought for a moment, then said, "Yes, Tom, I can. This is the most wonderful story I have ever heard along this line." And he told me this:

Years ago, two young men lived in the New England states. One came from a poor family. He and his widowed mother lived alone. The other was an only son of very wealthy people.

These two boys were both called into the service of their country in World War I and were placed in the same company. They became inseparable friends.

One day the poor boy got a letter telling him that his mother had died and he would now be alone in the world. The son of the wealthy family tried to console his buddy.

They continued their wonderful friendship. They went through several battles together.

Then one night in France the rich boy was seriously injured and lay dying on the battlefield. His poor friend crawled to his side, picked him up and held him in his arms as he died. The rich boy said to his friend, "Take off this blood-soaked shirt from my body. If God lets you live through all this, when you get back home, go to my father, give him my bloody shirt, and tell him that my dying request was that you be adopted as his son and become heir to all his wealth."

Some months later the war ended, and the poor soldier boy reluctantly approached the wealthy home. A butler came to the door and sought to turn him away, saying, "Since his son was killed, the master sees no one."

"But I have a message from his son," said the poor boy.

He was ushered into the palatial home. As the wealthy man and poor soldier stood together, he told the stricken father of his son's dying request. He then gave him the blood-stained shirt, and the two embraced each other and wept together, and the poor became a son of the rich!

Thank God, you, too, can come out of rags into riches, out of darkness into light, out of sin into eternal salvation through the precious blood of the Lord Jesus Christ. "...the blood of Jesus Christ his Son cleanseth us from all sin."

"Forasmuch as ye know that ye were not redeemed with corruptible things, as silver and gold, from your vain conversation received by tradition from your fathers; But with the precious blood of Christ, as of a lamb without blemish and without spot."—I Pet. 1:18, 19.

"The rich and poor meet together: the Lord is the maker of them all."

Chapter IV

Heaven's Warning or Hell's Destruction

First Prize Winning Sermon in Sword Evangelistic Sermon Contest, 1964

"But I will forewarn you whom ye shall fear. . . . "—Luke 12:5.

"And he said unto them, Take heed, and beware. . . . "—Luke 12:15.

Jesus was the greatest Preacher and Teacher the world has ever known. To be a great teacher, at least three things are essential. A teacher must know his subject, he must know his pupils, and he must believe what he teaches.

These things were all true of Jesus. He knew His subject: He was the Creator of everything animate and inanimate. He is the Author of life. He knew His pupils: with omniscience, He knew them. "He knew what was in man." He believed what He taught, because it was the truth, and He was the personification of the truth itself. "I am the way, the truth, and the life: no man cometh unto the Father, but by me." He believed what He taught and preached, because it came from the Father: ". . . but as my Father hath taught me, I speak these things."

Jesus preached with authority. His words were not like the faltering steps of a man uncertain of his way. Every word was like the blow of a hammer, the point of an arrow, or the blade of a knife.

"For he taught them as one having authority, and not as the scribes."

Jesus preached with simplicity. The greatest sermon ever delivered was the Sermon on the Mount. Its message is made up almost entirely of monosyllables. Jesus spoke in such a way as to make the way to Heaven plain.

He never confused His listeners with complicated expressions. It is no wonder that the Word of God says, "Never man spake like this man."

Jesus preached to the masses. "And the common people heard him gladly." Jesus reached the ear of the poor, the sinful, the neglected, the mistreated, the brokenhearted, the despised, the hopeless. He preached to the "down and out" and to the "up and out."

Jesus preached with sympathy and tenderness. He loved the people to whom He spoke—He loved them so much that He went to the cross and died for them, and for us. What tender invitations came from His lips!

"Come unto me, all ye that labour and are heavy laden, and I will give you rest."—Matt. 11:28.

"All that the Father giveth me shall come to me; and him that cometh to me I will in no wise cast out."—John 6:37.

He often wept as He preached. That sob in His voice was because of compassion and love in His heart. "And all bare him witness, and wondered at the gracious words which proceeded out of his mouth" (Luke 4:22).

He preached with power! Such power was evident in His words that it almost defies description. When He spoke, worlds came into being, life came out of nothingness, and celestial bodies were sprinkled in the heavenly expanse. When He spoke, angry waves became calm, and inflamed demons were cast out. When He spoke, His words made blind eyes to see, deaf ears to hear, and dumb lips to burst into praise. "And they were all amazed, and spake

among themselves, saying, What a word is this! for with authority and power he commandeth the unclean spirits, and they come
out'' (Luke 4:36).

Jesus preached the Scriptures, the Word of God, the saving
Gospel of light. Even some of the blind religious leaders of His
day recognized this, for they said to Him, ''Master, we know that
thou art true, and teachest the way of God in truth . . .'' (Matt.
22:16). No falsehood nor deceit ever fell from His pure lips.

Jesus preached with warning. He said, ''Beware'' and ''I will
forewarn you'' (Luke 12:1, 5). Jesus was an alarmist! The inflam-
mability of sin, the reality of Hell and the finality of eternity moved
in upon His soul and caused Him to warn people. His preaching
was like a waving red lantern: it was ''Stop, Look and Listen''
to all of His hearers.

Earnest warning is born of sincere love. Loving parents warn
their children against physical and moral danger. The more intense
the love, the more sincere the warning. Paul said, ''Therefore
watch, and remember, that by the space of three years I ceased
not to warn every one night and day with tears'' (Acts 20:31).

Jesus warned people and still warns them against all pitfalls and
subtle hazards that blight human hopes, damn souls and send
people to Hell. May Almighty God, who spared not His own Son,
help you to hear the warning voice of the Lord Jesus Christ
today. Oh, how the blessed Word of God pleads with people to
hear His voice, to heed His call, and be saved before it is too late!
''Wherefore (as the Holy Ghost saith, To day if ye will hear his
voice, Harden not your hearts, as in the provocation, in the day
of temptation in the wilderness . . .'' (Heb. 3:7, 8).

God says, ''To day''—not tomorrow, nor later; not when you
feel you have time, not when you are down and out, not when
you are at the end of the journey of life, but ''To day''! There
is an urgency in the voice of God as He pleads for your soul. God
would keep you out of Hell. ''Come now, and let us reason
together, saith the Lord: though your sins be as scarlet, they shall

be as white as snow; though they be red like crimson, they shall be as wool'' (Isa. 1:18).

Jesus is the Divine Flagman, the Heavenly Watchman, the One who weeps and warns of sin and its awful ruin.

At least seven great warnings are to be found in the eternal words of the Lord Jesus Christ.

I. HE WARNED AGAINST CHRIST REJECTION

When Jesus had saved and healed the poor, suffering man waiting on the pentagonal porch of the pool of Bethesda, the Jews sought to kill Him. In response to their hate and depravity, Jesus sought to love them, to save them. In John 5:24 He said, ''He that heareth my word, and believeth on him that sent me, hath everlasting life. . . .''

They would not hear His word! Like millions today, they turned a deaf ear to Him. He warned them that the day would come when they would have to listen, but then it will be too late.

''Marvel not at this: for the hour is coming, in the which all that are in the graves shall hear his voice, And shall come forth; they that have done good, unto the resurrection of life; and they that have done evil, unto the resurrection of damnation.''—John 5:28, 29.

You who are out of Christ will hear now and be saved or hear later and be lost. Make up your mind that somewhere, sometime, you will have to listen to God. No sadder words ever came from Jesus' heart than those of John 5:40, ''And ye will not come to me, that ye might have life.'' It is not that you *can*not come to Christ, but it is that you *will* not come to Him.

I remember a handsome young man with whom I pleaded about his soul. He was attentive and mannerly and listened to all I had to say. As I held him by his hand and begged him to be saved, it seemed as if the Holy Spirit impressed me that I would never be able to talk to him again. I was sure that, in spite of the fact that he was only nineteen years of age, it was now or never for his soul! He said to me what many have tragically said: "Preacher, I don't intend to go to Hell, and I do want to be saved someday, but I am just not ready tonight."

In spite of earnest, tender warning, he went away unsaved. There seemed to be such a feeling of finality about his refusal. In less than a month, he took his life with a gun and went out to meet God. I preached his funeral with a broken heart: I knew he had gone to Hell. "Ye will not come to me, that ye might have life."

How often Jesus warned! "He that believeth on him is not condemned: but he that believeth not is condemned already, because he hath not believed in the name of the only begotten Son of God" (John 3:18). If you will not hear, if you are yet in your sins and in unbelief, you are already condemned! You are on death row. Your judgment is as certain as God!

II. HE WARNED AGAINST LIVING AND DYING IN SIN

"Then said Jesus again unto them, I go my way, and you shall seek me, and shall die in your sins: whither I go, ye cannot come."—John 8:21.

Jesus never lets people live with a false hope. He warns that at the end of a sinful life is a Christless grave and an eternal Hell of awful torment. The greatest tragedy that could possibly befall a human being is to die in sin. As the tree falls, so shall it be. If you die in sin, there is no reprieve, no second chance, no higher court of appeals. Jesus once said to His audience, "Except ye repent, ye shall all likewise perish" (Luke 13:3). Jesus said it is REPENT OR PERISH!

To Nicodemus, on that night long ago, He said, "Except a man be born again, he cannot see the kingdom of God."

In Matthew 5:20 Jesus warned the multitude who listened to Him preach from the mountainside, "Except your righteousness shall exceed the righteousness of the scribes and Pharisees, ye shall in no case enter into the kingdom of heaven.'' So the message is clear, the instructions plain. There is no Heaven without repentance, no forgiveness without the spotless righteousness of Christ.

Many die in their sins in spite of much warning. Self-deceived Judas waited too long for tears and repentance and lost his soul. He heard the sermons of Jesus, saw His miracles and went to Hell over all of it. The second thief on the cross heard Jesus pray for His enemies, heard Him speak tenderly to His mother, heard Him promise forgiveness to the other thief. He was so close he could hear the dripping blood from the cross of Christ, but he went to Hell. He would not listen, would heed no warning, so he 'died in his sins.'

At least eight times in Genesis 5 is this expression, ''and he died.'' That is the tragic history of the human race. You must die; you cannot escape an encounter with death. ''And as it is appointed unto men once to die, but after this the judgment.'' The road to Hell is paved with good intentions. Be saved now. Do not die in your sins, for that means you are forever lost and without hope!

Today hear His voice.

III. HE WARNED AGAINST REFUSING TO HEAR AND OBEY THE WORD OF GOD

"Therefore whosoever heareth these sayings of mine, and doeth them, I will liken him unto a wise man, which built his house upon a rock: And the rain descended, the the floods came, and the winds blew, and beat upon that house; and it fell not: for it was founded upon a rock. And every one that heareth these sayings of mine, and doeth them not, shall be likened unto a foolish man, which built his house upon the sand: And the rain descended, and the floods came, and the winds blew, and beat upon that house; and it fell: and great was the fall of it.''—Matt. 7:24–27.

It is a most solemn thing to think of the millions of poor lost souls in the history of the human race who never heard the Gospel. Millions, no doubt, are already in Hell because Christians, churches and preachers failed to evangelize to the ends of the earth.

The Bible, however, teaches that even "they are without excuse" (Rom. 1:20). If they be without excuse, who have never heard as you have heard, what awful torment must await the man or woman who hears the story of God's love over and over again but refuses to heed and obey!

The Gospel is a Gospel of grace, but there is a divine command in it. That command is to believe the Gospel and believe on the Person and finished work of the blessed Son of God. God's Word is clear and unmistakable as to the awful fate of those who refuse to hear and believe the Bible.

"And to you who are troubled rest with us, when the Lord Jesus shall be revealed from heaven with his mighty angels, In flaming fire taking vengeance on them that know not God, and that obey not the gospel of our Lord Jesus Christ: Who shall be punished with everlasting destruction from the presence of the Lord, and from the glory of his power."—II Thess. 1:7-9.

Remember that Jesus warned that the awful storms of life would inevitably come to every human being. I have seen them come to people of all walks of life: the rich and the poor, the learned and the unlearned, the young and the old. Storms come in the form of sorrow, loss of health, ambitions and dreams of a lifetime suddenly broken upon the rocks of misfortune.

Be not deceived; the storms will come. The storm will beat and blow upon your little boat of life when you least expect it. The only security is the Rock of Ages. A life founded upon anything less is a life built upon sinking, shifting sand.

What will you do when the rains descend and the floods rise and the winds beat vehemently? What will you do when sorrow overtakes you, despair defeats you and leaves you broken and undone? What will you do in the evening of life when hair is gray

and loved ones have long since departed and your loneliness is
only exceeded by your tears of remorse? What will you do when
friends you thought were as stable as stone prove as fickle as the
wind and you are swallowed up with frustration and delusion? What
will you do when the body is worn out and disease has taken its
toll? What will you do when at the bitter end of life's little day
you must meet the Christ of bloody Calvary whom you have
ignored and despised?

Oh, in God's name, I plead with you today to hear Him, to heed
His warning!

IV. HE WARNED AGAINST FALSE PROPHETS

There is absolutely no question that many are lost because they
are being misled by false prophets who are lost themselves. All
preachers are not saved. There will be many of them in Hell. All
the preachers who followed Jesus were not saved. For instance,
Judas, who went on healing campaigns and was elected treasurer
of the apostolate, was not a born-again believer. He was lost and
is now in Hell.

Jesus taught and warned that many millions would be eternally lost because of being deceived by some religious leaders. Matthew 15:14 tells us, "And if the blind lead the blind,
both shall fall into the ditch."

It has always been thus. Satan himself is religious. He was an
"angel of light" even before he was cast out of Heaven. He has
his preachers, just as Jesus has His.

*"For such are false apostles, deceitful workers, transforming
themselves into the apostles of Christ. And no marvel; for Satan
himself is transformed into an angel of light. Therefore, it is no
great thing if his ministers also be transformed as the ministers
of righteousness; whose end shall be according to their works."*—II
Cor. 11:13-15.

These preachers of Satan are educated and, in many instances, refined, cultured and moral. They are "ministers of righteousness"; but it is "self-righteousness," not the righteousness of Christ. The righteousness of Christ can only be obtained through self-condemnation and the total recognition of evil and depravity in the human heart. The righteousness of Christ is "of God and by faith."

Many religious leaders today are "ignorant of God's righteousness, and going about to establish their own righteousness." Millions are being engulfed in this satanic and subtle program. Are you one of them? Are you sure that you have salvation in Christ Jesus? Or do you just have religion? Are you positive that there was a time and place when you were made a new creature in Jesus Christ?

God speaks plainly about these "blind leaders of the blind."

"His watchmen are blind: they are all ignorant, they are all dumb dogs, they cannot bark; sleeping, lying down, loving to slumber. Yea, they are greedy dogs which can never have enough, and they are shepherds that cannot understand: they all look to their own way, every one for his gain, from his quarter."—Isa. 56:10, 11.

In speaking of these lost religious leaders, Jesus said, "Beware of false prophets, which come to you in sheep's clothing, but inwardly they are ravening wolves. Ye shall know them by their fruits. Do men gather grapes of thorns, or figs of thistles?" (Matt. 7:15, 16).

You cannot recognize them by their dress, because they wear "sheep's clothing." You cannot recognize them by their speech, because they say, "Lord, Lord." You cannot discern them by their sphere of operation, because they are men who have "crept in unawares," and they operate in the realm of religion and even within the true church and deceive many.

Are you one of those being deceived? By their fruits you shall know them. Does your preacher have the fruits of the new life in his life? Does he lead others out of sin and darkness into light and salvation and the new birth? I have seen hundreds of religious but lost church members claim Christ and get saved in the many years I have been in the ministry.

O friend, be sure you have Christ in your heart and the Holy Spirit in your life. Don't be deceived and led to Hell by a blind religious leader. May God help you to be saved.

V. HE WARNED AGAINST SELF-DECEPTION

"Not every one that saith unto me, Lord, Lord, shall enter into the kingdom of heaven; but he that doeth the will of my Father which is in heaven. Many will say to me in that day, Lord, Lord, have we not prophesied in thy name? and in thy name have cast out devils? and in thy name done many wonderful works? And then will I profess unto them, I never knew you: depart from me, ye that work iniquity."—Matt. 7:21-23.

Many will be self-deceived into believing they are saved, until it is too late. What an awful day of awakening when they hear Jesus say, "I never knew you"! Though active in religious work and going through much religious ritual and ceremony, yet they are never saved! The Bible says that even many who sincerely believe they are saved are actually lost. "There is a way which seemeth right unto a man, but the end thereof are the ways of death" (Prov. 14:12).

Many have said to me, "Preacher, if a person is sincere in what he believes, don't you believe he will get to Heaven?"

I don't believe that is true. You can be sincerely wrong. When a mother gave her baby a dose of poison instead of a dose of medicine, she was sincere in believing it was medicine; but did her sincerity keep her baby from dying?

Some time ago I received a letter from a young woman twenty years of age, a pastor's daughter. She was away from home, working in another city, and had been listening to our radio broadcast. Actually, she was hearing the Gospel for the first time in her life, she said. Her father-pastor was a modernist and didn't preach the Gospel himself. She wrote to tell me that she had never personally accepted the Lord Jesus Christ as her own Saviour. She, like many others, had been deceived into believing that she was not bad enough to need salvation.

How different is the Bible account of man's need!

"There is none righteous, no, not one."—Rom. 3:10.

"For all have sinned, and come short of the glory of God."— Rom. 3:23.

"But we are all as an unclean thing, and all our righteous-nesses are as filthy rags; and we all do fade as a leaf; and our iniquities, like the wind, have taken us away."—Isa. 64:6.

Jesus told the heart-searching parable of the ten virgins, five wise and five foolish, or five lost and five saved. The five who were lost were self-deceived and didn't know they were lost until they heard the midnight cry of the coming bridegroom. Then it was too late; the door was shut, and they were on the outside. Poor, deluded young women—they lost their chance of Heaven. Oh, self-deception, that tool of the Devil! How many have been slain therewith!

"To day if ye will hear his voice, harden not your hearts."

VI. HE WARNED AGAINST COVETOUSNESS

"And he said unto them, Take heed, and beware of covetous-ness: for a man's life consisteth not in the abundance of the things which he possesseth."—Luke 12:15.

The love of something material or tangible has damned many souls. The love of prestige, popularity, friends, clothes and many good things, even necessary things, often stands between you and Jesus.

Jesus asked, "What shall it profit a man, if he shall gain the whole world, and lose his own soul?"

Jesus told us of one who gained the world but lost his soul.

One night a rich farmer sat in his beautiful home and wrestled with a problem. He had so much of this world's goods that his barns would not hold them all. "What shall I do?" he cried, as he reviewed his earthly riches and neglected his eternal soul. His love for the cheap, temporal things of life drowned his sense of values and made him act like a fool.

Little did he know it, but death stalked his home that night. And in the midst of abundance, he died with no heavenly wealth and lost his soul.

The tragic account of his death is found in Luke 12:20: "But God said unto him, Thou fool, this night thy soul shall be required of thee: then whose shall those things be, which thou hast provided?"

Like a cankerous sore, covetousness ate at his inner man. Like a blood-thirsty animal, it sapped away his sense of values. Covetousness caused him to substitute time for eternity, the temporal for the eternal, Hell for Heaven, Satan for Christ. What a poor bargain he made! He gained the world, but he lost his soul.

"For the love of money is the root of all evil." I once heard a man say that becoming a Christian cost him $50,000 a year in crooked business. He is one in a million. Most men would rather have the $50,000 a year than to have Jesus. Jesus has often been sold for less. Such was the case of Judas who sold Him for thirty pieces of silver.

In a large southern city where I was preaching some years ago, a millionaire was being buried. The funeral procession was on its way through town, and there were many observers. Two men stood at a service station. One commented, "I wonder how much he left." The other deliberated for a moment, then said, "He left it all!" How true! There are no pockets in a shroud. What folly to gain the world and lose your soul! Jesus warned against covetousness.

VII. HE WARNED AGAINST HELL

Jesus spoke often of Hell. He warned people of its awful reality, its terrible torment, its haunting memories, its unending suffering. "But I will forewarn you whom ye shall fear: Fear him, which after he hath killed hath power to cast into hell; yea, I say unto you, Fear him" (Luke 12:5).

Those who say there is no Hell or that it will not last forever or that God is too good to let people suffer in Hell, either have not heard what Jesus said about it, or they will not believe it.

"And if thy hand offend thee, cut it off: it is better for thee to enter into life maimed, than having two hands to go into hell, into the fire that never shall be quenched: Where their worm dieth not, and the fire is not quenched. And if thy foot offend thee, cut it off: it is better for thee to enter halt into life, than having two feet to be cast into hell, into the fire that never shall be quenched: Where their worm dieth not, and the fire is not quenched. And if thine eye offend thee, pluck it out: it is better for thee to enter into the kingdom of God with one eye, than having two eyes to be cast into hell fire: Where their worm dieth not, and the fire is not quenched."—Mark 9:43–48.

Five times in this one passage Jesus says, "The fire is not quenched."

In tenderness and tears and with a broken heart, Jesus was constantly warning people about Hell.

It is said that one night while a faithful preacher of the Gospel was preaching in an open air meeting and warning his audience about being lost and cut off from God forever, a young man began to heckle him. "Where is Hell?" the skeptic cried. "At the end of a Christless life," the preacher answered.

My friend without Christ, where will you spend eternity? Will you not listen to Jesus and be saved?

Some months ago a personal friend of mine, a devoted Christian, was witnessing to a young man in a service station. The young man said, "I know you are right, but I am too busy and having too good a time right now to think about being a Christian. Maybe later, but not now."

When his car was serviced, he started the motor and drove about two miles. While rounding a curve, he lost control of the car, struck a tree, and was instantly killed. Five minutes earlier a faithful witness warned him that he might lose his soul. He was two miles from Hell, but he would not listen to the warning! He was a five-minute ride from the torment of Hell, but he was having too good a time to listen. He refused the warning and, tragedy of tragedies, is now in Hell.

Jesus went to a bloody cross and bore your sins. He arose from the grave to keep you out of Hell. He is at the throne of God pleading for your soul. Hear His earnest warning; listen to His tender invitation.

"Come unto me, all ye that labour and are heavy laden, and I will give you rest."—Matt. 11:28.

"All that the Father giveth me shall come to me; and him that cometh to me I will in no wise cast out."—John 6:37.

"For whosoever shall call upon the name of the Lord shall be saved."—Rom. 10:13.

"And the spirit and the bride say, Come. And let him that heareth say, Come. And let him that is athirst come. And whosoever will, let him take the water of life freely."—Rev. 22:17.

Chapter V

Life's Sinking Sun

(Preached at Emmanuel Baptist Church, April 15, 1959)

"Woe unto us! for the day goeth away, for the shadows of the evening are stretched out."—Jer. 6:4.

As a country boy, how well do I remember hearing my mother and others gathered about the old-fashioned pump organ in the large farmhouse singing:

> **Life's evening sun is sinking low;**
> **A few more days and I must go**
> **To meet the deeds that I have done,**
> **Where there will be no setting sun.**

For many of our acquaintances, "life's evening sun" has long since sunk below the horizon of earth. This sobering verse from the Bible describes the state of all living, ". . .the day goeth away, for the shadows of the evening are stretched out."

Nothing is so beautiful and tranquil as a sunset at the close of day. How clearly does my memory afford me a picture now of the close of day on the farm where I spent my boyhood: tired farmers coming from the fields singing, cattle moving slowly toward the barn, birds subduing their mellow song preparing for the night, shadows stretching out across the plowed fields and the sun sinking low in the West as God prepared to close the doors of the day and draw the shades of night about us. God uses this as an illustration to show to men the brevity of life, the passing of opportunity and the certainty of death.

May God's Holy Spirit burn with inescapable conviction the awful fact of Jeremiah's sermon to the sinning Jews, ". . .the day goeth away."

I. THE DAY OF OPPORTUNITY DRAWS TO A CLOSE

How often does the Bible bring before sinners the fact that God gives men an opportunity to be saved, then in His own time, closes that opportunity. This was true of the antediluvians of Noah's day. God said, "My spirit shall not always strive with man, for that he also is flesh: yet his days shall be an hundred and twenty years" (Gen. 6:3).

The wicked antediluvians turned a deaf ear to God's warning, laughed at God's preacher and finally suffered God's judgment. When God closed the door of the ark, shutting Noah and his family in, He closed forever the opportunity to be saved for that generation.

God has given you the opportunity to be saved. Woe unto the foolish one who trifles away that opportunity!

The blind man of Jericho heard the multitude cry out, 'Jesus passes by'; and he cried out, "Have mercy on me." He realized this was his moment of great opportunity to have his eyes opened. We read in Luke 19:1, "And Jesus entered and passed through Jericho." Zacchaeus said to himself, *I must see Him as He passes through, for He may never pass this way again.*

When Paul reasoned before him of righteousness, temperance and judgment to come, little did Felix know that his day of opportunity to be saved was about to pass away forever. "Go thy way for this time; when I have a convenient season, I will call for thee," said he. That convenient season never came, and Felix now suffers in Hell with his awful memory of a wasted life.

When the doors of the prison cell closed upon God's preacher

Paul as he left the presence of Felix and Drusilla, the doors of opportunity closed forever upon this wicked ruler who heard the message of the glorious Gospel of salvation but turned a deaf ear and lost his soul.

Many times have we seen this same tragic occurrence.

Some years ago I was asked to preach at a great New Year's Eve service here in the state of Michigan. As I prayed about my message, it seemed as if my heart and mind were filled with Luke 12:20, "But God said unto him, Thou fool, this night thy soul shall be required of thee: then whose shall those things be, which thou hast provided?"

That text proved to be most appropriate. Little did I realize that that very afternoon a man for whom I had prayed and to whom I had witnessed and whom I had tried to win, said to his wife, "I am going to hear Tom Malone preach tonight; and when he gives the invitation for sinners to be saved, I am going to walk down that aisle and give my heart to Jesus."

That night he sat about five rows from the front. The congregational singing was over. The quartet sang, "When They Ring the Golden Bells." The words ring in my ears to this moment: "When our days shall know their number." I read the Scripture and quoted my text, "Thou fool, this night thy soul shall be required of thee." Suddenly this man arose to his feet, walked out of the church and fell dead in a pool of blood on the steps!

God said, "This night thy soul shall be required of thee." He waited thirty minutes too long. It is often said, "Opportunity knocks but once." But as far as being saved is concerned, opportunity has knocked many times. You have sat through revival campaigns, and God has spoken to you. Your Christian friends have prayed, wept and pleaded with you to be saved. Remember that "the day [of opportunity to be saved] goeth away, for the shadows of the evening are stretched out."

Jesus said in Revelation 3:20, "Behold, I stand at the door, and knock: if any man hear my voice, and open the door, I will come in to him, and will sup with him, and he with me.'' Don't you hear Him knocking today at the door of your heart? Let Him come into your life.

A word here would certainly be in season to Christians. We so often "fumble the ball" and let opportunities to win souls slip through our fingers. Remember Jesus said in John 9:4, "I must work the works of him that sent me, while it is day: the night cometh, when no man can work." The time is short for Christians to win souls. Oh, that we would be alert to every opportunity to witness.

Some time ago I received a tract in the mail which told of J. Wilbur Chapman's experience with a lost man. Mr. Chapman was a great soul winner, and no doubt thousands are in Heaven today because of his ministry in reaching the lost. But Mr. Chapman himself tells of one soul he failed to win.

He was asked to go to a hospital to see an unsaved, sick man. As he was about to enter the room an attendant in the hospital asked him, "Whom do you wish to see?"

Mr. Chapman told him. The attendant said, "This patient is very nervous. If you talk to him about his soul, it may make his condition even worse. Why not visit with him just a moment or two, get acquainted, then come back tomorrow and tell him how to be saved?"

Mr. Chapman took the attendant's advice and didn't press the claims of Christ upon the lost man but left and promised to return the next day.

When he came back, the same attendant was cleaning the hospital room and said, "If you came to see the man you saw yesterday, he is not here."

"Where is he?"

"He died a few minutes after you were here yesterday."

I wonder how many souls whom our Saviour loved and for whom He died will be in Hell because of the negligence and unconcern of professing Christians.

II. THE DAY OF GOD'S GRACE DRAWS
TO A CLOSE

This particular age or dispensation is spoken of in various ways in the Bible. It is referred to as the age of the Gentiles or that period of time in which the Jews are dispersed over the face of the earth and the world is under Gentile dominion. Jesus referred to this age in Luke 21:24 as the "times of the Gentiles." Technically, perhaps, these "times of the Gentiles" began when the Jews were taken captive by the Babylonians about 700 years before Christ came into the world, but this is the age when the Gospel is being sent to the multitudes and not just to the Jews. This is the day when "whosoever shall call upon the name of the Lord shall be saved."

This age or this day is also spoken of in the Bible as the dispensation of God's grace. Paul referred to this age in his Ephesian letter (3:2) as "the dispensation of the grace of God which is given me to you-ward."

Yes, through His kindness and love, God offers to deal with sinners in grace. He will pardon and forgive the repenting and believing sinner. This age of grace and unmerited favor of God toward sinners is fast coming to its close. ". . . the day goeth away, for the shadows of the evening are stretched out."

This age is also spoken of in the Bible as the "last day" or "last days." The Prophet Joel marked out this age as beginning at Pentecost and ending with the coming of the Lord Jesus in glory and power. In Joel 2:28-32 we read:

"And it shall come to pass afterward, that I will pour out my spirit upon all flesh; and your sons and your daughters shall prophesy, your old men shall dream dreams, your young men shall see visions: And also upon the servants and upon the handmaids in those days will I pour out my spirit. And I will shew wonders in the heavens and in the earth, blood, and fire, and pillars of smoke. The sun shall be turned into darkness, and the moon into

blood, before the great and the terrible day of the Lord come. And it shall come to pass, that whosoever shall call on the name of the Lord shall be delivered: for in mount Zion and in Jerusalem shall be deliverance, as the Lord hath said, and in the remnant whom the Lord shall call.''

It was prophesied that . . .

(1) . . .the Holy Spirit would come "in the last days" (so interpreted in Acts 2:17), which was on the day of Pentecost.

(2) . . .this glorious event would usher in the day of "whosoever shall" (vs. 32).

(3) . . .this age would end with signs and wonders in the heavens, which refer to the second coming of Christ.

Sometimes people ask, "Brother Malone, don't you believe we are in the last days?" We have been in the last days since the day of Pentecost; and we see evidence in the Bible, in the church, in the Jew, and in the world and its affairs that this age is drawing to a close and "the shadows of the evening are stretched out."

Paul said in II Corinthians 6:2, "Behold, now is the accepted time; behold, now is the day of salvation." If you will not bow the knee to Jesus, acknowledge your sin and your need of Him in this day of God's grace, you will never be saved. It is now or never for sinners.

We preachers are often asked if sinners will have an opportunity to be saved after Jesus has taken His bride, the church, out of the world. The book of Revelation says a select number of Jews will be saved and also "a great multitude, which no man could number"; but there is not the slightest bit of indication that one who hears the Word of God in this age of grace and refuses it, will ever be saved after Jesus comes. When the trumpet sounds for the rapture of the saints, it will be blowing "taps" for the unrepenting sinner who has allowed this age to come to a close with his heart still hardened against God.

Jesus told in Matthew 25:11-13 the parable about five foolish girls who waited too late. The bridegroom came, the door was shut, and they were left outside. "And while they went to buy, the bridegroom came; and they that were ready went in with him to the marriage: and the door was shut" (vs. 10).

What tragic words—"and the door was shut"! They had waited too late! The door to the kingdom was shut in their faces, and they were outside. No amount of pleading and crying could cause the door to open. They had crossed the deadline; they had stayed out too late; and when they finally decided they wanted in, they found the door shut forever in their faces.

The men of Noah's day made the fatal mistake of staying out too late! God looked upon their wickedness and lust and said, "I will destroy man whom I have created from the face of the earth." When God looked upon the violence, immorality and rebellion of Noah's day, it "grieved him at his heart." When God saw the wickedness of man was great, it repented the Lord that He had made man.

But even in the judgment of the Flood, God's grace and mercy shine forth. God gave man one hundred and twenty years before judgment and destruction came. During those years, Noah faithfully declared God's message. People had time to repent, to turn to God and be saved; but they didn't want to be saved. They said, 'There's lots of time. Let us eat, drink and be merry.' They loved their sin too much to give it up.

When the ark was completed and the hour of crisis had arrived, we read that God said, "Noah, Come thou and all thy house into the ark; for thee have I seen righteous before me in this generation" (Gen. 7:1). We read, "And they that went in, went in male and female of all flesh, as God had commanded him: and the Lord shut him in" (vs. 16). When God shut that door, it sealed forever the eternal doom of the wicked men and women of that generation! Their sun had set. They had ignored the sinking sun, the lengthening shadows, the approaching shades of night.

Millions are making the same mistake today. They are procrastinating and putting off the all-important matter of being saved before it is too late. God pleads with sinners, "Come now, and let us reason together...though your sins be as scarlet, they shall be as white as snow; though they be red like crimson, they shall be as wool" (Isa. 1:18). The psalmist says in 119:59, 60, "I thought on my ways, and turned my feet unto thy testimonies. I made haste, and delayed not to keep thy commandments."

How well do I remember an incident that took place when I was about fourteen! At that time I was attending a rural high school some twelve miles from the farm where I lived. Spring had come, and school was soon to be over. I used to walk over a mile every morning—summer and winter—to catch the school bus, then ride about twelve miles. That year I was finishing the ninth grade; and, naturally, I felt quite well educated!

When the last day of school arrived, I was certainly happy. We were to have some special exercises; it was to be a big day. I wouldn't have missed it for anything.

But that morning I failed to watch the clock, and the time slipped by before I knew it. When I realized it was getting late, I ran out of the house and down the railroad track for over a mile to the highway where I was to catch the bus. There is little doubt in my mind but that I set a new world's record that morning for running the mile; but, of course, that is unofficial!

When I finally came to the highway, I looked down the road and saw the bus going away from me. Frantically I waved my arms and screamed to the top of my voice, but to no avail. I was left behind! I was too late! I missed the last day of school, and my heart was broken. Slowly I walked back home with tears streaming down my cheeks. I kept repeating to myself, "Too late! Too late!"

Friend, don't delay any longer. Settle this matter today. Don't stay out of the kingdom until it is too late. When Jesus comes and the door is shut, your hope of being saved will forever be gone.

III. THE DAY OF GOD'S LIGHT WILL TURN TO SIN'S DARKNESS

God sends His sweet rays of salvation's light to the sinner. Any opportunity to trust Christ is another opportunity to step by faith out of darkness into light.

Early one morning as the sun came up over Jerusalem and dispelled the darkness of night, Jesus said, "I am the light of the world: he that followeth me shall not walk in darkness, but shall have the light of life" (John 8:12). In the great Sermon on the Mount, Jesus said to the Christian, "Ye are the light of the world. A city that is set on an hill cannot be hid" (Matt. 5:14). God has made it possible for sinners to see the light of salvation and be saved.

Satan hates that light, and his work is to keep the unsaved from seeing it. Paul speaks of Satan's efforts to hide the light in II Corinthians 4:3, 4:

"But if our gospel be hid, it is hid to them that are lost: In whom the god of this world hath blinded the minds of them which believe not, lest the light of the glorious gospel of Christ, who is the image of God, should shine unto them."

The tragic thing about the sinner and the light of the Gospel is that someday that light will shine no more. Light rejected is sometimes light recalled or withdrawn. In John 8 where Jesus proclaimed Himself as the light of the world, the light was rejected; and the chapter ends by saying that "Jesus hid himself." Light rejected is often light withdrawn.

I made several trips to a man's house to try to lead him to Christ. He was eighty years old and had a heart as hard as stone. He criticized God, Christians and churches. He mentioned preachers who had done wrong and criticized me for speaking on tithing at Emmanuel Baptist Church.

I took others with me at different times and continued to try to win him but with the same results.

One day I went to his home; and when he refused to let me in, I stuck a tract through the screen door and asked him if he would please read it after I left. "No, I won't promise to read it; but I will promise you that as soon as I close the door, I'll throw it in the trash."

Some days later I went back to his door and asked, "Is Mr. Jones here?" A young man answered, "No. He has gone to another state."

When I left that day, I knew that the day he closed the door with a gospel tract in his hand, he had shut out the light forever. Oh, that sinners would step out into the light while the sweet light of God's love and grace still shines upon them!

"Woe unto us! for the day goeth away, for the shadows of the evening are stretched out."

IV. THE DAY OF EARTHLY LIFE
DRAWS TO A CLOSE

No wonder the psalmist prayed, "So teach us to number our days, that we may apply our hearts unto wisdom" (90:12). He had seriously contemplated the brevity of life and said that life was like grass, 'green in the morning and withered in the evening'; 'like a tale briefly told'; like a life that is 'soon cut off.' James says (4:14), "For what is your life? It is even a vapour, that appeareth for a little time, and then vanisheth away." What could be more fragile, more temporary than vapor? Solomon warned, "Boast not thyself of to morrow; for thou knowest not what a day may bring forth."

How foolish for one to say, "I have plenty of time; there is no use to get so excited about this thing."

Some years ago as I was reading the Bible and praying one Sunday afternoon, I felt impressed to go see a man whom I had witnessed to and prayed for, yet hadn't been able to win. He was forty years of age, over six feet tall and a fine specimen of manhood.

I can see him now as he came to the door of his home. He shook my hand, smiled and invited me in. I said to him, "Jim, God laid you on my heart today, and I could not rest until I had come one more time to try to get you to trust Christ and be saved."

He said to me, "Brother Malone, I am glad you are interested in my soul. As a preacher, you ought to be interested in getting people saved; but I'll tell you frankly, I'm not ready. I'm not an old man. My health is good. I have other things on my mind at this time."

No amount of pleading on my part nor the tears and prayers of his good wife, who sat with us in the living room of his nice home, could change him. I left with a heavy heart. I had hoped to win him that day.

Just four or five days later his wife called and screamed into the phone, "Jim's dead, Brother Tom! Jim's dead! And he has gone to Hell because he wouldn't listen to you when you tried to get him saved."

I preached his funeral and watched them put the flowers on his grave. I saw his wife and children turn and walk from the cemetery, knowing they would never see him again.

"*. . .the day* [of earthly life] *goeth away, for the shadows of the evening are stretched out.*"

God's Word says, ". . .it is appointed unto men once to die, but after this the judgment."

One Sunday morning as I was giving the invitation and people were being saved, a young married man fairly ran down the aisle, grasped my hand and said, "Mr. Malone, I want to be saved right now. I heard you tell of this young man who was here last Sunday, heard you preach, was spoken to by one of your personal work-ers but wouldn't get saved. I heard you tell how this week he was burned to death in his truck and went out to meet God unprepared. I surely don't want that to happen to me. I'm not going another day without getting saved!''

How wise that young man was to get saved, and how foolish the other young man was who gambled with his soul and lost! He waited too late. He procrastinated. He put it off. He ignored the setting sun and lengthening shadows and went to Hell as the result of his folly.

Friend, Christ died for you. He says in John 6:37, "Him that cometh to me I will in no wise cast out." Proverbs 27:12 says, "A prudent man foreseeth the evil, and hideth himself; but the foolish pass on, and are punished." How foolish to pass on over God's warnings and refuse His mercy and grace! Proverbs 29:1 says, "He, that being often reproved hardeneth his neck, shall suddenly be destroyed, and that without remedy."

May God help you to believe and be saved. "Too late! Too late!" will be the cry of many in Hell who, like Agrippa, were almost persuaded.

"...the day goeth away, for the shadows of the evening are stretched out."

Chapter VI

Jesus, the Door of Salvation

(Preached at the Emmanuel Baptist Church, Sunday morning, September 17, 1961)

"I am the door: by me if any man enter in, he shall be saved, and shall go in and out, and find pasture."—John 10:9.

It would be a blessed and sweet experience to any Christian to go through the four Gospels—Matthew, Mark, Luke and John—and read the verses where Jesus said, "I am."

"I am the water of life." Thank God, He is!

"I am the way, the truth, and the life."

"I am the bread of God come down from heaven."

Here in John, in His divine effort to make the way of salvation clear, Jesus says to all men of all ages everywhere, "I am the door: by me if any man enter in, he shall be saved, and shall go in and out, and find pasture."

There are three doors mentioned in the first nine verses. In verse 1 is the door of the sheepfold; in verse 7, the door of the sheep; in verse 9, the open door of salvation.

I speak today on "Jesus, the Door of Salvation": "I am the door: by me if any man enter in, he shall be saved."

I had an experience some years ago that I shall never forget. I was sitting in a church service by one of the greatest men of God I have ever known. He now is in Heaven with the Lord. He was a man of great experience. He was in his seventies then and had been preaching nearly since he was just a young man. He had won thousands of people to the Lord. If I were to call his name, most of you would know him.

While the young preacher was preaching and I was listening, that old veteran of the Faith, that old battle-scarred preacher, reached over, put his hand on my knee and said, "Tom, don't ever quit preaching on the great but simple texts of the Bible."

After the service was over, he explained what he meant. "In this day and time, many no longer preach on John 3:16. Many do not preach on Romans 6:23. Tom, don't ever quit preaching on the great but simple texts of the Bible that make it plain and clear how to be saved."

My heart's desire is to make the way to Heaven plain and clear, so plain, so clear that no one in this church will ever be able to say, "It was not explained to me; no one tried to make it clear."

Jesus said, "I am the door: by me if any man enter in, he shall be saved."

I saw the remains of some of the old-fashioned sheepfolds in the Holy Land. They were merely a little wall about six feet high, made in a circular fashion. If you walked around one of them, you would find the opening to be about six feet long. There is no gate—never had been and never will be—in a sheepfold. When the night came, the shepherd called, and the sheep knew his voice; and when he walked into the sheepfold, the sheep followed. Then as night came on, the sun went down and the moon came up. With his shepherd staff, that shepherd lay across that opening, about six feet in width. The door to the sheepfold was not an inanimate object; it was not a gate; it had no latches, no hinges. The door of the sheepfold was a person. Jesus said, "I am the door: by me if any man enter in, he shall be saved."

I have thought of five simple truths about that door.

I. JESUS IS THE ORDAINED DOOR

God has ordained Jesus as the door. Before God ever put a star in the heavens, before He ever flung this world from His omnipotent fingers, God ordained that Jesus Christ, His Son, born of a virgin, conceived of the Holy Ghost, who would live among men, die on a cross and arise from the grave—God in Heaven ordained before the foundation of the earth that His Son would be the ordained door. We read in I Peter 1:18-20:

"Forasmuch as ye know that ye were not redeemed with corruptible things, as silver and gold, from your vain conversation received by tradition from your fathers; But with the precious blood of Christ, as of a lamb without blemish and without spot: Who verily was foreordained before the foundation of the world, but was manifest in these last times for you."

So Jesus, dying on the cross for our sins, was ordained of God. See Calvary as a part of God's plan; then you see what it is all about. Calvary was no accident. Jesus was not just a martyr. Rather, He said:

"Therefore doth my Father love me, because I lay down my life, that I might take it again. No man taketh it from me, but I lay it down of myself. I have power to lay it down, and I have power to take it again. This commandment have I received of my Father."—John 10:17, 18.

Calvary, the death, the suffering, the blood of Jesus on the cross—these were no accident, no afterthought, not something that God thought of two thousand years ago. It was something planned in the eternal councils of God back in the beginning of eternity. It was ordained of God that Jesus should suffer and die. Every drop of blood, every bit of spit, every drop of sweat, every hand cuffed upon His blessed face, every thorn in His brow, the spear in His side, His feet nailed to a cross—all were planned in the heart of a tender, gracious God before the world was ever made.

Oh, may you see today that He is the ordained door! He was ordained to die. Oh, I hope you see that Calvary, redemption, salvation, eternal life and Heaven cost God something.

"For God so loved the world, that he gave . . . ." No one ever gave more; no one ever could. God gave a spotless, innocent Son, One without blemish, without sin, to suffer, bleed and die on a cross.

A preacher was telling of two sisters who dearly loved one another. Both were married. One day God gave one of them a dear little baby. The other sister said, "I'll take care of you and the baby until you are back to health again." The sister with the little baby moved with her kind sister into the home in Beaumont, Texas.

One day a fire broke out in that home, and the sister ran up the steps where mother and baby were asleep in the bedroom. She got the little baby and took her out and laid her in the yard. By now the neighbors had come and had taken over. The sister rushed into the house and called her sister's name as loud as she could call. She saw her sister crumple and faint at the top of the stairs. She rushed up the stairs; and when she reached the top, flames began to enfold behind her. She didn't know what to do; she was trapped. Dragging her sister, she ran to the bedroom, raised the window, got hold of her sister and tumbled her out the window. She fell one story down to the lawn. A hip was broken; but a few weeks later she had healed, and her life had been saved.

But the sister who saved the mother and baby was trapped. By the time she jumped out the window, her body had been frightfully burned, and she was suffering terribly. In a few days she died.

That sister saved a baby and a woman but at the cost of her own life.

You want to remember that salvation is only possible, Heaven is only possible, eternal life is only possible, because Someone came out of Heaven who was willing to give, willing to lay down His life. God ordained it that way, and there is no other way but through the shed blood of Jesus.

You don't go to Heaven head first; you go heart first. If you think you can think your way into Heaven, you have another thought coming. You don't go head first; you go heart first.

This Bible says, "For after that in the wisdom of God the world by wisdom knew not God, it pleased God by the foolishness of preaching to save them that believe" (I Cor. 1:21). There is only one way, a blood way, a way of a cross.

It is not by education. You don't go head first; you go heart first. Jesus said, "I am the door," the ordained door. In Acts 10:42 we read, "And he commanded us to preach unto the people, and to testify that it is he which was ordained of God to be the Judge of quick and dead." He is ordained according to the Scriptures.

II. JESUS IS THE ONLY DOOR

Jesus is the only door; there is no other. The Bible beautifully illustrates this in the Old Testament. One day God said to Noah, who was righteous in God's sight, 'I want you to build an ark.'

No one in this day could build a ship with more proper dimensions than the ark. It was built according to God's pattern. But that ark, three stories high, had but one door. There was only one way into it and only one way out of it.

One day the people of God came out of the land of Egypt and were taken to the land of Canaan. God said to them, 'I want you to build a Tabernacle.' I am not talking about the Temple in Jerusalem but the portable Tabernacle, erected and taken down as this great army of redeemed people moved from Egypt, the type of the world, into Canaan, a type of the Christian life. The Tabernacle had but one door. Every offering came through that door. Every priest went through that door. Everyone who entered into the outer court where the congregation met, went in one door.

All through this Bible, God states that there is only one door. Jesus said in John 14:6, "I am the way, the truth, and the life: no man cometh unto the Father, but by me." One way. One door.

In olden days, streets were called "ways." Jesus said, "I am the way"—the road to Heaven. Sometimes folks say, "Well, we are going different ways, but we are all going to the same place." They quote that old, timeworn expression, "All roads lead to

Rome.'' No, they don't! All roads around Rome do not lead to
Rome. Some may lead to Florence, some to Venice. And all roads
don't lead to Heaven. Jesus said, ''I am THE DOOR.''

I say to you, there is only one way to get to Heaven, and that
is to walk through that door just like I walked through it. You
must walk through that door just like every sinner walks through
it. There will be no pride go through it. There will be no rebellion go through it. There will be nobody but sinners go through
that door. ''I am the door: by me if any man enter in, he shall
be saved.''

If the Christian people, the saved people, you church members,
would let that truth dawn on you, some of you would not let the
sun go down until you had made an all-out effort to win your loved
one to Jesus Christ, the ONLY door.

I was reading recently of something that actually happened years
ago on the New England coast. There was a shipwreck. (There
used to be a lot more then than now.) A lifeboat came to shore.
A crowd had gathered, not knowing who was in the boat. Someone in the crowd asked, ''Were all the men rescued?'' The captain of the ship was in the lifeboat. He answered, ''All but one
man. He was late getting off. The ship was about to go down,
and the lifeboat was full, so we had to leave him. One man is still
out there somewhere, hanging on a bit of wreckage.''

There stood a young man there on the shore, John Holden. His
mother stood near him. John Holden began to take off his clothes.
He was going after that man. He got into that lifeboat with the
captain, but his mother cried, ''John, don't go! John, don't go!''

As John Holden and the captain of the ship rowed that lifeboat
out to sea, John heard his mother cry out, ''Your dad, four years
ago, was drowned in the sea. Your brother went to sea a year ago,
and we haven't heard from him since. Don't go, John!''

But John rowed out through the waves and the storm. After
awhile that little lifeboat came back, and three men were now in
it. It is said that John Holden stood up in the boat, looked toward

the shore and heard someone cry out, "Did you get the man?"

John Holden said, "We got the man. And tell Mother it is Will."

Oh, my friends, suppose that mother had persuaded that son not to go. Suppose he had not risked his life to try to save the lone man holding to that wreckage. Her own boy Will would have gone down and drowned.

O God, help Christians to see that He is the ONLY door. There is no other hope for your children. There is no other way for your family. There is no other way for people to be saved.

"I am the door: by me if any man enter in, he shall be saved, and shall go in and out, and find pasture."

III. JESUS IS THE OPEN DOOR

Jesus is the open door. That door has not been closed for nearly two thousand years. In John 6:37 we read, "All that the Father giveth me shall come to me; and him that cometh to me I will in no wise cast out." The door is always open. "He that cometh to me"—rich or poor, white or black, up and out or down and out, learned or unlearned, wise or unwise, sick or well—"I will in no wise cast out."

Jesus is the open door: the open door to Heaven, the open door to happiness, the open door to freedom.

In John 8:36 Jesus said, "If the Son therefore shall make you free, ye shall be free indeed." There are not many free people in America. This is a nation of slavery. People are slaves to the god of gold, slaves to the god of pleasure. We talk about the land of the free and the home of the brave, yet there never has lived in the history of mankind a more enslaved people than live in America today. There is no freedom except that found in Jesus Christ.

IV. JESUS IS THE OPPORTUNE DOOR

Jesus is the opportune door. What do I mean by that?

Sometimes people take the attitude that they will be saved when they want to be. That is not necessarily true. You may be in this church this morning, and you may say to me, "Mr. Malone, I don't want to be saved today. I'd rather be saved a week from now or a month from now."

A week from now you may be here and have the same desire, the same emotions and willingness, and you may walk down the aisle and be saved. But you may not. You may be dead a week from now. You may be dead an hour from now. You may be dead a moment from now. I have seen the ambulance back up to the church door where I was preaching and take people away who lost their lives in that church service.

Jesus is an opportune door. What do I mean by that? I mean exactly what Isaiah 55:6 says, "Seek ye the Lord WHILE HE MAY BE FOUND, call ye upon him while he is near." "...while he may be found." Seek Him when? When He is speaking to you. Seek Him when loved ones are weeping over and praying for you. Seek Him when the Gospel is being preached. Seek Him while you have your right mind. Job said, "Because there is wrath, beware lest he take thee away with his stroke" (Job 36:18).

I have seen folks who rejected Jesus be smitten with a stroke of insanity; then they didn't have the mind nor faculties to accept Him. "Seek ye the Lord while he may be found, call ye upon him WHILE HE IS NEAR."

When the dark hour comes and you lie somewhere on a hospital bed in a coma and can't speak a word nor recognize loved ones—He won't be near you then. He will be near you only when you have your right mind and when you, in good sense, can accept Him as your personal Saviour.

He is an opportune door. Let me prove it to you.

In chapter 25 of Matthew, Jesus told a parable of how it would be when He came back again. In verse 10 we read, "And while they went to buy, the bridegroom came; and they that were ready went in with him to the marriage: AND THE DOOR WAS SHUT.''

There came a day when God instructed that the door of the ark be closed. And the Bible says, ''The Lord shut him in.''

When the Lord shuts the door, no man can open it. When the Lord opens it, no man can shut it.

Jesus is an opportune door.

One of the saddest stories in the Bible is found in Judges, chapter 19. I have often asked myself and the Lord, *Why is Judges 19 in the Bible?*

It is a very strange chapter. It tells of a man and his wife who were traveling on their way to the Lord's land. They spent the night in the home of an old man in a certain city.

Evil men, sons of Belial, came to the door of the old man who entertained them and said, ''Bring forth the man that came into thine house, that we may know him.'' They were going to beat the door down and tear the house down if their wish wasn't granted.

Instead, this old man allowed his wife (concubine) to be given over to the wicked men of the city of Ephraim. The Bible says that all that night they ''knew her'' and abused her. When morning came, they let her go. Now verses 26, 27:

''Then came the woman in the dawning of the day, and fell down at the door of the man's house where her lord was, till it was light. And her lord rose up in the morning, and opened the doors of the house, and went out to go his way: and, behold, the woman his concubine was fallen down at the door of the house, AND HER HANDS WERE UPON THE THRESHOLD.''

She thought, *If I can just get through the door.* As the sun arose, she came and fell at the door; and her hands were on the threshold. When daylight came, they came from the house and spoke to her and said, ''Up, and let us be going.'' But no answer came. Why? She was as cold as a stone in death.

That is an awful picture, but it is God's picture of someone striving and struggling when it is too late to get through the door. He is an opportune door.

Now and then we use the expression in our preaching, "It is now or never." That must be true, because people hear the Gospel and do not believe and lose their souls.

"I am the door: by me if any man enter in, he shall be saved, and shall go in and out, and find pasture."

V. JESUS IS AN OPTIONAL DOOR

You don't have to be saved. No one can make you be a Christian. No one made me be saved. People prayed, witnessed and preached. I saw how Christians lived. No one made me be a Christian; and no one can make you be a Christian.

Folks have said to me sometimes in our visitation work, "Now, Mr. Malone, I don't want to have this forced on me." I agree with them. You cannot make a person be saved. It is a voluntary act.

Jesus is an optional door. You don't have to take it. You can go ahead and bow to the god of intellectualism or the god of gold or the god of pleasure or the god of religion. You don't have to take Jesus. You can bypass Him.

Jesus says, "I am the door: by ME if any man enter in, he shall be saved."

You don't enter in through a catechism. You don't enter in through a denomination. You don't enter in through an ordinance. Jesus said, "BY ME." He is saying that the gate to Heaven is a glorious Person.

I read a lot of things that Jesus said. I can almost take the words and wring the tears and the blood from them. I read where He turned one day and asked, "Will ye also go away?"

I read another expression that fell from the lips of Jesus. There is no sadder expression because in this expression the souls of men hang in the balance between Heaven and Hell. Jesus one day looked at a crowd and said, "And ye will not come to me, that ye might have life."

That is why people are not saved—not because they *can*not, but because they *will* not.

He is an optional door.

Back hundreds of years before Calvary, Joshua put it like this: "...choose you this day whom ye will serve" (24:15). It is a matter of choice.

I close with this story that I am sure is true. There was a young girl in her teens in Glasgow, Scotland, many years ago. She, like many today, was tired of home, tired of restraint, tired of discipline, tired of prayer and the Bible. One day she decided to go to the city and find a job and make a life for herself.

She went. Weeks turned to months, and months turned to years. The big city life got in her blood, and she went down. She became a street walker and a woman of sin.

One day an old woman came to Glasgow. There were two rescue missions in the city. The old lady went to both. At each place she took out of a brown paper bag a picture of herself. She said to the superintendent of each mission, "I'd like you to hang this on the wall."

One said, "That is a strange request. Why?"

"I have a daughter in this city, and I want her to come home. I have prayed and wept and spent one sleepless night after another. If you will put this picture on the wall of your mission, maybe someday or some cold night she will come to this house of God and see it and know that I still love her."

Down at the bottom of the picture the mother had written, "Come home. I love you still."

The superintendent of each mission said, "I will do it."

The old mother prayed and wept. Months went by.

One night a young fallen girl walking the streets of Glasgow saw the mission and heard the singing. Cold, hungry, destitute and friendless, she went in. Sitting there, all of a sudden she looked toward the wall and saw a picture—a picture of an old, gray-haired mother of many years. She saw the tenderness and love that was in her face. She looked at the picture and said, "O God, can it be!"

When the service was over, she went to the picture and stood with tears rolling down her cheeks as she read what was underneath: "Come home. I love you still."

That night she started home. In the wee hours of the morning, she came to the home that she had left long ago, walked up onto the porch, laid her hand upon the knob; and the door immediately opened. Fear gripped her heart. She thought something was wrong, for her mother would never leave the home unlocked.

She ran in and ran as fast as she could through the darkened rooms to the bedroom where her mother was. There she found her with eyes wide open.

She said, "Mama, I've come home! When I found the door unlocked, it frightened me. I thought something was wrong, that someone had entered the house and molested you."

The mother looked at her daughter and said, "No, my dear. From the day you left this house to wander in sin, the door has never been locked."

They prayed together that night, and God settled it all.

The door to Heaven is open. It is optional. You can come and look in today and go on your way. No one will force you into it. But it is the only door and the only way to Heaven.

"I am the door: by me if any man enter in, he shall be saved, and shall go in and out, and find pasture."—John 10:9.

Enter Now

Dear reader, after reading Dr. Malone's simple and stirring sermon on "Jesus, the Door of Salvation," you must understand Jesus is the only access to salvation. But how wonderful it is that the door stands wide open to whosoever will!

There was an impassable wall of sin between us and God. When Jesus died on the cross, the Bible says He became sin for us. In other words, Jesus made Himself part of the wall between us and God; and by becoming sin for us, He became a door of access.

On the cross He paid our sin penalty. He died in our place and then rose from the grave with power.

Now everyone who trusts Jesus as Saviour enters into everlasting life with his sins forgiven and a home in Heaven.

But Jesus is the only access. God says anyone who tries to enter another way is a thief and a robber. By that God is telling us that to try to get to Heaven any way other than through Jesus only worsens our situation.

If you will not enter by Jesus, you must remain eternally separated from God; and that means that, when you die, you will go to Hell forever.

But now you still have opportunity to trust Jesus, and He is near. If you will trust Him as your own Saviour, pray this simple prayer, telling Him you will:

> Dear Lord Jesus, I know I am a sinner deserving Hell. Thank You for loving me and dying for me on the cross to pay my sin debt. I do now trust You and You only to forgive my sins, save my soul and give me a home in Heaven. Please help me to live for You and be a good Christian. Amen.

If you have now trusted Jesus as your Saviour, please fill out the decision form on the next page and send it to me. I have a beautiful book I want to send you free of charge that will be a blessing and help to you as you begin the Christian life.

Decision Form

Dr. Shelton Smith
Sword of the Lord
P. O. Box 1099
Murfreesboro, TN 37133

Dear Dr. Smith:

I read the sermon by Dr. Tom Malone, "Jesus, the Door of Salvation." After reading that sermon, I have trusted Jesus as my Saviour. I would appreciate receiving the free book you promised that will help me as I begin to live the Christian life.

Date _____

Name _____

Address _____

_____

Chapter VII

"Not Far From the Kingdom of God"

(Preached at Emmanuel Baptist Church, Pontiac, Michigan, Sunday morning, August 28, 1960)

"And one of the scribes came, and having heard them reasoning together, and perceiving that he had answered them well, asked him, Which is the first commandment of all? And Jesus answered him, The first of all the commandments is, Hear, O Israel; The Lord our God is one Lord: And thou shalt love the Lord thy God with all thy heart, and with all thy soul, and with all thy mind, and with all thy strength: this is the first commandment. And the second is like, namely this, Thou shalt love thy neighbour as thyself. There is none other commandment greater than these. And the scribe said unto him, Well, Master, thou hast said the truth: for there is one God; and there is none other but he: And to love him with all the heart, and with all the understanding, and with all the soul, and with all the strength, and to love his neighbour as himself, is more than all whole burnt-offerings and sacrifices. And when Jesus saw that he answered discreetly, he said unto him, Thou art not far from the kingdom of God. And no man after that durst ask him any question."—Mark 12:28–34.

Jesus said this to a sincere man, "Thou art not far from the kingdom of God."

Jesus didn't say that this man was IN the kingdom and imply that he was saved. He said that he was NEAR to being saved.

The man to whom Jesus had directed this statement had asked Him a question. Read all of Mark 12 and a few verses from the preceding chapter which actually are attached to it, and you find men—most of them the enemies of Christ—had asked Him four questions in this part of the Bible.

1. In the first question, they questioned His authority. Jesus had gone into the Temple and found it desecrated. Finding the tables of the moneychangers and those who sold doves for sacrificial purposes, He made a cord and cleansed the house of God. They asked, "By what authority doest thou these things?" (11:28).

2. In Mark 12:14 the Pharisees questioned His integrity: "Is it lawful to give tribute to Caesar, or not?" They wanted to find out whether Jesus was honest enough to obey civil law.

3. The Sadducees questioned the doctrine of Jesus; for in Mark 12:19-23 they said:

"Master, Moses wrote unto us, If a man's brother die, and leave his wife behind him, and leave no children, that his brother should take his wife, and raise up seed unto his brother. Now there were seven brethren: and the first took a wife, and dying left no seed. And the second took her, and died, neither left he any seed: and the third likewise. And the seven had her, and left no seed: last of all the woman died also. In the resurrection therefore, when they shall rise, whose wife shall she be of them? for the seven had her to wife." (The practice of a woman having two or more husbands at the same time was called the doctrine of polyandry.)

Jesus gave them correct doctrine when He said, "For when they shall rise from the dead, they neither marry, nor are given in marriage; but are as the angels which are in heaven."

Here they questioned His doctrine and intelligence. They wanted to find out what Jesus knew about the Bible, the Word of God, and about the Law.

4. This next man mentioned is both a scribe and a Pharisee. A scribe worked on the Bible to translate the verses. A Pharisee was a very religious person. He asked Jesus in Mark 12:28, "Which is the first commandment of all?"—a most controversial question.

The Jews argued much about this question. They had 365 prohibitions—one for every day in the year—which divided the Bible and added to it. Each of these prohibitions read like this, "Thou shalt do no. . . ." The Jews had 228 commandments, and they believed there was one for every part of the human body. All this great group of religious people, many of whom were lost, argued and debated about what was the greatest commandment in all the Bible.

When this man came to Jesus, he questioned his Bible intelligence. He wanted to know if the Son of God really knew what the greatest commandment in the Bible was. Jesus said:

"The first of all the commandments is, Hear, O Israel; The Lord our God is one Lord: And thou shalt love the Lord thy God with all thy heart, and with all thy soul, and with all thy mind, and with all thy strength: this is the first commandment."

No one knows the depth of what Jesus meant when He said, "Thou shalt love the Lord thy God with all thy heart, and with all thy soul, and with all thy mind, and with all thy strength."

Jesus stated that the second commandment is like unto the first: "Thou shall love thy neighbour as thyself."

There is man's relationship to God and to others. When this man who had asked the question heard Jesus give this intelligent answer, he said, "Well, Master, thou hast said the truth."

I am told that in the Greek writing of the New Testament, the true meaning is that this man who asked the question got very excited. He literally jumped up and down and said, "Wonderful! Master, You have answered the question admirably." This scribe said, 'This truly is the greatest commandment, to love God with all the heart and soul and strength.'

Jesus looked at him and declared, "Thou art not far from the kingdom of God."

I wish that the truth from that simple statement of Jesus could grip your heart.

I never read this verse but what I think of a story I read in our newspaper a few years ago.

There was a plane coming into O'Hare Field in Chicago, the busiest airport in the world. One beautiful night a mother and a dad stood watching the planes arrive. The plane number they were meeting had been called. They stood out on the observation deck and watched for it to come in. They saw the lights flashing in the darkness. On that plane was their soldier son, coming home from the war in Korea, whom they had not seen in a long time. The mother and father held hands; their hearts were happy. "Just think! In two more minutes our son will be here!"

All of a sudden there was an awful explosion. That plane carrying their son literally crashed and disintegrated. Not one lived to tell what happened.

Every time I think of that story I think, *Almost home, but he never made it!*

That is the picture of many men and women—almost saved but eternally lost. "Thou art not far from the kingdom of God."

Whether this applies to you or not, think with me along five simple, brief lines for a few moments.

Why is it that God could look down on a man's soul and say to him, though he is lost, "You are not far from the kingdom of God"?

I. THIS MAN KNEW THE FUTILITY
OF LAW-KEEPING

Here is a man who had studied and translated the Bible. Here is a man who worked in it all the time. From reading that Bible, he found that no man can be saved by keeping the Law, something many people have never found out. There are people today who, if you examined their teaching and doctrine, hope to be saved by keeping what they call the law of God. Whether it is a certain day or a certain service, their whole salvation depends on law-keeping.

Two verses will prove that no man could be saved by so-called keeping of the law of God. So many people today actually believe that is the only way we can be saved, that it is a gospel of works, not of grace.

Paul said in Romans 3:19, 20:

"Now we know that what things soever the law saith, it saith to them who are under the law: that every mouth may be stopped, and all the world may become guilty before God. Therefore by the deeds of the law there shall no flesh be justified in his sight: for by the law is the knowledge of sin."

I ask you this question: Do you believe we are under Old Testament law? Of course you don't. You don't offer a lamb upon an altar as a sacrifice. You don't observe the Jewish ritual of the Old Testament. Our Bible teaches that by "the deeds of the law" no one can be justified.

A young man, a member of my church, came to my office with a young lady he desired to marry. He and the young lady each had a Bible. They were a wholesome and clean-looking couple.

The man said, "Brother Malone, we have a problem, so we have come to you for help and advice."

I asked what their problem was.

He said, "We love each other and want to be married, but she is of a different religion."

The girl had her Bible. She had read it and had marked in it. She knew where to find what she wanted. As she sat with that Bible in her lap in my office, she questioned me out of the Book of God. She asked me about the keeping of the law. When I tried to answer her, I got nowhere. You can't explain the Bible to one unsaved.

Finally, I felt led to ask this sincere, humble, lovely, young lady, with a Bible that she owned, loved and read, a pointed question: "Are you saved?"

"If you mean, have I been baptized, no."

"I don't mean that. I mean what Jesus meant when He said, 'Except a man be born again, he cannot see the kingdom of God.' "

"No, I have never been born again."

May God help us to see that one cannot be saved by the observance of the law. Any intelligent person who is not prejudiced can see from the first few verses of I Timothy 1 that we are not saved by keeping the law.

". . .the law is not made for a righteous man, but for the lawless and disobedient, for the ungodly and for sinners, for unholy and profane, for murderers of fathers and murderers of mothers, for manslayers, For whoremongers, for them that defile themselves with mankind, for menstealers, for liars, for perjured persons, and if there be any other thing that is contrary to sound doctrine."

Here are about thirteen of the most horrible, damnable sins people have ever committed; these are the people for whom the law was intended.

This man said to Jesus, 'To love God with all your heart is greater than all the sacrifices and burnt-offerings and all the Old Testament law.' Jesus said, 'You are close to the kingdom of God.'

II. THIS MAN SAW THE EMPTINESS OF ORDINANCE OBSERVANCE WITHOUT CHRIST

Many people who want to be baptized and observe the ordinances never amount to anything spiritually. They want Christianity without Christ, salvation without repentance, separation without self-denial. They want the same old crowd and the same old habits.

They want to do exactly what they please and still be called good Christians.

There is no Christianity without Christ. There is no salvation without repentance. There is no separation without self-denial and sacrifice. Many people want the honor of God without humility. There is no such thing.

This man, by his answer to Christ, showed that he did not believe that you could be saved by observing the so-called Old Testament Law.

You ask, "Why are you talking about that?"

There are two New Testament ordinances—the ordinance of baptism and the ordinance of the Lord's Supper. Many good people believe you must be baptized in order to be saved. I have never helped one of them yet by taking the verses they take and trying to explain them. But for every verse about which there seems to be a doubt as to what it means concerning baptism, I can take you to twenty that have no doubt about it. If you are honest and believe the Bible, I can prove to you that baptism never has saved and never will save and is not efficacious as far as salvation is concerned.

Romans 6:4, 5, which doesn't deal with an unsaved man but with one who has already accepted Christ, says:

"Therefore we are buried with him by baptism into death: that like as Christ was raised up from the dead by the glory of the Father, even so we also should walk in newness of life. For if we have been planted together in the likeness of his death, we shall be also in the likeness of his resurrection."

In reference to baptism, God uses the words "burial" and "planted." I ask you, Do you bury a person in order to kill him? Any sane and honest person knows you do not. Why do we bury people? Because they have already died. That is the only reason. This is in reference to baptism. You don't baptize a person to put him to death spiritually; you baptize only a person who has died spiritually and has been saved. Doesn't that make sense? You don't bury people to kill them; you bury them because they have already died. You don't baptize people to save them; you plant them because they have already been saved. Those who will not accept that truth are biased, prejudiced and not sincere; and there is no help coming to them.

Many good people believe that you must observe the ordinance of the Lord's Supper to be a Christian. But that ordinance is never for the unsaved. Even when Jesus instituted it in chapter 13 of John, before it ever ended and the truth was consummated, Judas had left and was lost. Only true believers observed the table of the Lord.

In I Corinthians 11:26 is this wonderful truth, "For as often as ye eat this bread, and drink this cup, ye do shew the Lord's death till he come." Every time we observe the Lord's Supper, we look in two directions. "Ye...shew the Lord's death"—looking backward; "till he come"—looking forward. When the believing Jew observed it, he looked backward to his deliverance from Egypt by the blood of the lamb, and he looked forward to the coming of the Son of God to die. For the Jew, the passover supper was both commemorative and prophetical—commemorative in that it looked backward to deliverance from Egypt and prophetical in that it looked forward to the coming of the Lamb of God.

No person has the right to sit at the Lord's table unless he can look backward and claim on Calvary a finished work and look forward and say, "When Jesus comes, I know He is coming for me."

When this man proved that he had no confidence and put no dependence and no hope in the keeping of the Law and the observance of ordinances, Jesus said, "Thou art not far from the kingdom of God."

III. THIS MAN KNEW HIS NEED

I don't know what he ever did about it—the Bible does not say—

but he was convicted of his need. You cannot be saved until you know your need.

I am getting so weary of these folks who are always picking out the faults of other Christians. Everyone has faults.

Don't you get aggravated with these folks who, when you start talking to them about the Lord and about being saved and living a holy life, stop you and say, "I knew a man once who claimed to be a preacher and he did so and so"? I'd like to say to that person, "Why, you sorry good-for-nothing: if you could only see yourself, you would start bawling right now. The very idea of your ever sitting in judgment on anyone! You were born in sin, with a sinful nature. Your heart and mind are depraved. You think unclean thoughts. You've spoken bitter words. Your whole mouth is an open sepulchre. Your feet have run onto mischief. You are full of sores from head to foot. How dare you sit in judgment on anyone!"

God says, 'Let every mouth be stopped.' Put your hand over your mouth and cry out, "O God, I am guilty, guilty, guilty!" God can do business with people who feel that way.

Here is a man who is convicted of his need.

When my aunt and uncle visited me a few weeks ago, I asked my aunt about a certain young lady who, twenty years ago in August, was in a revival meeting where I was preaching and where many people were saved, including many of my dear loved ones.

I saw that woman in that audience get under conviction. She literally became as white as snow, so white that it looked as though there was not one drop of blood in her body. She laid hold on the seat in front of her and gripped it so hard that her knuckles looked like there was no flesh on them. She shook like a leaf moved by the wind.

A fine Christian woman went to her and pleaded with her and said, "I've prayed for you, and I want you to be saved. Won't you come?" That young woman never answered. I went myself and begged and pleaded with her, but she didn't come.

Twenty years later I asked my aunt, "What ever happened to that girl?"

My aunt said, "She has gone from bad to worse. She has had a broken home and has gone downward, downward, downward for twenty years."

If you come up to the threshold of salvation and have God deal with your immortal soul and see the glories of Heaven and the horrors of Hell and you turn back, it will be hard for you ever to come back. For every time you say no, you harden your heart and steel the fiber of your soul against God. When the Holy Ghost of God convicts you, you are not far from the kingdom if you will act upon that conviction.

IV. HE KNEW THE WORD OF GOD WAS TRUE

This man complimented Jesus when he said, "Well, Master, thou hast said the truth." He believed there was one God and only one. He believed that one ought to love God with all his soul, with all his strength and to love his neighbor as himself. I think it would be safe to say this man believed that whatever the Bible says is true. This didn't mean he was a child of God and on his way to Heaven. Many people know that the Bible is God's Book yet are not saved because they have not done what it tells them to do in order to be saved. One must believe on the Lord Jesus Christ in order to be saved. I do think that this man's attitude about the Word of God had something to do with Jesus' saying, "Thou art not far from the kingdom of God." No one can be saved apart from the Word of God. The Bible makes this clear. "So then faith cometh by hearing, and hearing by the word of God," says Romans 10:17. In speaking of the Scriptures, Jesus said, "...and they are they which testify of me" (John 5:39). I know men are sinners because the Bible says they are. I know Jesus died on the cross, bearing the sin of the world, because the Bible says He did. I know He rose from the grave because the Bible says so. No one can be saved apart from the Bible. And those who do not believe the Bible is God's Word are not saved. One is born again by the Word of God. "Being born again, not of corruptible seed, but of incorruptible, by the word of God, which liveth and abideth for ever" (I Pet. 1:23).

I have asked many people, when trying to lead them to Christ, "Do you believe that the Bible is true and that it is the Word of God?" Many times they answer, "Yes, I have always believed the Bible." But just believing the Bible doesn't make you a Christian. You must believe on the Lord Jesus Christ as your own Saviour.

A man in Philippi asked Paul and Silas, "Sirs, what must I do to be saved?" And they answered, "Believe on the Lord Jesus Christ, and thou shalt be saved, and thy house." He believed and was saved, and his family was saved; then they were all baptized. This is God's way to be saved.

V. THIS MAN WAS CLOSE TO JESUS

This man could have reached out and touched Jesus. I wish I could get that close to Him. I wish I could see Him as He was then. Oh, I think I would fall at His feet and put my arms around them. That man got his information straight from the mouth of Christ, for he talked to Jesus. Oh, how Jesus loved him! Soon Jesus was to be led up the hill of Calvary to die on the cross for the sins of that man. I think if he would have let Him, Jesus would have put His arms around him and said, "Son, thy sins be forgiven thee."

I don't know what happened; but when he came up to the door, I think every angel in Glory and God the Father and God the Son said, "Come on inside." Whether he came or not, only God knows.

When I was six, we lived in Memphis, Tennessee. A young man who was very nice to me lived in the same apartment house with my family. I liked him very much.

One day he said to my mother, "I'd like to visit my mother

and father on the old ranch in Texas where I was raised, and I'd like for Tom to go with me.'' My mother thought about it for a few hours and finally said, "He can go.''

There are so many things about that trip that I remember. First, I remember the car, a one-seater. The only way you could tell whether it was coming or going was to watch it awhile! I remember the lunch my mother fixed, which she put in a suit box. It was literally filled with little brown southern biscuits and chicken, fried just the way I like it.

We started out before daylight. I was so excited that I never leaned back until twelve o'clock! I sat right on the edge of the seat looking out the window.

But I remember a sad experience. We came to a river, and there was no bridge. There was a ferryboat, and the man who operated it lived in a house near the river. The sun was dropping beneath the sky; and the young man kept saying, "Tom, we'll be home soon. We'll see the ranch, my mother and dad, and the horses. Supper will be ready.''

I was so excited that fatigue didn't mean a thing. We came to the river. The ferry was tied up, and no one was around. This young man said, "He lives right there in that house. You wait here, and I'll go get him; then we'll go on across the river.''

It is as vivid to me as if it happened five minutes ago. There was the river in front (a muddy river), and the sun was going down. This young man went up the hill to the house. The ferry man came out on the porch. They talked awhile. I could see their heads shaking. Finally my friend came back. He got in the car and said, "Tom, he closes the ferry at a certain hour; and he says if he goes across, it will be dark before he can get back. He won't take us.''

He sat there and told me, "Now just across the river and down the road and around the curve is where Mom and Dad live. In five minutes we would be there if we could just get across the river.''

We sat there and saw the sun go down. We heard the crickets, saw the lightning bugs, and darkness came. Disappointed and sad, all night long we slept in that car. I remember that I cried. Just across the river—but we couldn't make it.

Today many a human soul is just across the river. The sun is going down. Darkness is coming. "Not far from the kingdom," yet still lost. On the other side, loved ones, every angel in Heaven, God the Father and God the Son are crying, "Come in. Come on in. Don't wait until it is too late."

A thief died and went to Hell when Jesus died. No doubt that all through eternity he is going to cry out, "Almost saved, but lost! Almost saved, but lost!"

Another thief died that day, but he was saved. Forever he will say, "Almost lost, but saved! Almost lost, but saved!"

"Thou art not far from the kingdom of God."

But You Can Step Into the Kingdom of God Today

Here are some great facts that every sensible person surely knows.

First, you are a sinner: "All have sinned, and come short of the glory of God." Since that is true, then every one of us needs Jesus Christ as Saviour.

Second, God loves us sinners. He sent Jesus to die for us and pay our sin debt so He could righteously forgive and save us. God wants to save you. Jesus died for you.

Third, you can be saved in a moment if you will simply trust Jesus Christ, surrender to Him, come to Him in your heart right now and depend on Him to save you. Remember that He said, "For God so loved the world, that he gave his only begotten Son, that whosoever believeth in him should not perish, but have everlasting life." If you want to be saved, you can be. I beg you to trust Him now and thus step into the kingdom of God!

Chapter VIII

The Wonderful Words of Jesus

(Preached in the Emmanuel Baptist Church, Sunday morning, May 18, 1969)

"It is the spirit that quickeneth; the flesh profiteth nothing: the words that I speak unto you, they are spirit, and they are life."—John 6:63.

"...thou hast the words of eternal life."—John 6:68.

These verses lead me to this subject, "The Wonderful Words of Jesus."

Both Peter and Jesus made a statement about these words. Jesus said, "...the words that I speak unto you, they are spirit, and they are life." He says, 'They are not of the flesh; they are not of the world. They are spirit, and they are life.' Then, Simon Peter testified, "...thou hast the words of eternal life."

If you were to take out of your red-letter edition of the Bible every verse written in red—the words that actually fell from the lips of the Lord Jesus Christ Himself—and put them in one book or pamphlet, it would be a small pamphlet. While on earth, Jesus did not actually speak a great many words in comparison to the rest of the Bible. Yet out of those pages of the pamphlet would be the greatest words ever spoken.

Thousands of volumes have been written on what Jesus said. One great man of a few generations ago wrote eight volumes on the words of Jesus alone, and each volume contained four hundred pages—3,200 pages of deep spiritual theological deliberation on the few words Jesus said.

"The words that I speak unto you, they are spirit, and they are life." I would say that these words have provoked more thought than all the words that ever fell from the lips of people, from the hour of Adam even until now. These words have provoked more thought than all the words of all the prophets of all the rest of the Bible. Of all the politicians who ever rang forth their convictions, and of all the potentates and kings who have ever spoken in the history of the world, none have provoked more thought and affected more behavior and changed more lives than the words of Jesus Christ.

If anyone would ever speak of himself as many times as Jesus spoke of Himself, he would become the most unliked and obnoxious character in the world. Jesus many times said, "I am." He said, "I am the door." He said, "I am the way." He said, "I am the water." He said, "I am the bread." He said, "I am the truth." He said, "I am the life." In spite of the fact that He pointed to Himself in His conversation, they are the most wonderful words ever spoken.

Many times He expressed Himself by saying, "I will." Yet, in spite of His firm will, these words by Jesus are the most wonderful words ever spoken. ". . .the words that I speak unto you, they are spirit, and they are life." It is like the wonderful old song we sing:

> Sing them over again to me,
>   Wonderful words of Life;
> Let me more of their beauty see,
>   Wonderful words of Life.
>
> Christ, the blessed One, gives to all,
>   Wonderful words of Life;
> Sinner, list to the loving call,
>   Wonderful words of Life.

> Sweetly echo the gospel call,
> Wonderful words of Life.
> Offer pardon and peace to all,
> Wonderful words of Life.

Why are the words of Jesus the most wonderful words that have ever fallen upon human ears?

I. WONDERFUL IN THE COMMENT THEY RECEIVE

First, they are wonderful in the comment they receive.

His first public message is recorded in Luke 4, when Jesus steps forth and says, "The Lord...hath anointed me to preach the gospel." He began to preach it and tell it—the first public message He ever gave—and when He had finished, we read these words, "And all bare him witness, and wondered at the gracious words which proceeded out of his mouth."

Oh, gracious words that lift burdens, dry tears, forgive sins and change lives—wonderful words of Christ! When He gave His first public message, people wondered at His "gracious words." One time when He was teaching, they said, "He taught them as one having authority, and not as the scribes." The Pharisees and chief priests one time sent officers to "take" (arrest) Jesus. They listened to Jesus, then came back. The officers had not arrested Him, and they didn't bring Him back. The enemies of Jesus wanted to know why. Well, as the officers listened to Him, their lives and hearts and opinions about Christ were changed. They came back and said, "Never man spake like this man" (John 7:46). They had never heard any words like these.

Again, in Luke 4:36, they spoke of His wonderful words: "And they were all amazed, and spake among themselves, saying, What a word is this! for with authority and power he commandeth the unclean spirits, and they come out."

The words of Christ are wonderful in the comment that they received.

I like to read of great preachers. Nothing in this world is greater than spiritual, powerful, Holy Ghost preaching—nothing other than the Word of God itself. I think of Jonathan Edwards who, a few decades ago, preached that famous message, "Sinners in the Hands of an Angry God." His words were such sparks of fire from the anvil of God that people said, "Oh, Mr. Edwards, stop such preaching lest God kill us all!" Such conviction came upon them.

E. Howard Cadle's mother listened to Paul Rader preach the Word of God. As he preached, Mrs. Cadle said, "I could see a halo about his head, almost a white light, as the power of God rested upon him."

Some years ago I listened to Dr. Bob Jones, Sr., in his prime. For two hours and twenty-six minutes he preached on "Follow Me, and I Will Make You Fishers of Men." I sat on the edge of my seat. When he finished his sermon, I wept because I didn't want him to stop after two hours and twenty-six minutes. The words flowed from the fountainhead of God. There came from his lips such a wonderful message! But his words were not like the words of Jesus.

"*. . .the words that I speak unto you, they are spirit, and they are life.*"

II. WONDERFUL BECAUSE OF THEIR WISDOM

Wonderful words! Why? Wonderful because of their wisdom. Men may have education; but unless they know the teaching of Jesus, they cannot possibly have the greatest wisdom man can ever experience.

We read in Isaiah 50:4, "The Lord God hath given me the tongue of the learned, that I should know how to speak a word in season to him that is weary." Jesus testified prophetically in this verse that the Lord had given Him the tongue of the learned that He might know how to speak a word in season to him who is weary.

Jesus knows what to say to you. Jesus knows your need.

He has the right message for you.

John 8:5 says, "Now Moses in the law commanded us, that such [the woman taken in adultery] should be stoned: but what sayest thou?" Her accusers brought her to Jesus in the Temple, flung her at His feet and said, "Master, this woman was taken in adultery, in the very act. Now Moses in the law commanded...but what sayest thou?"

Suppose someone would bring a person to me about whom the Bible says, "Stone this person to death," and say to me, "Now Dr. Malone, what do you say?" I would be in a dilemma. There would be no way out. I would have to say, "If the Bible says it, then that must be done."

But not Jesus. He wrote upon the ground as though He wasn't listening. When they persisted, Jesus had some words to say: "He that is without sin among you, let him first cast a stone at her." Being pricked in their own conscience, beginning with the eldest to the youngest, they left Jesus standing alone. He looked at that shivering, quivering, defeated, soiled woman lying on the floor and said, "Woman, where are those thine accusers? hath no man condemned thee?" She said, "No man, Lord." He said, "Neither do I condemn thee." That sounds like a condonation, but it isn't— "Neither do I condemn thee: go, and sin no more."

The Old Testament demanded her death. The Christ who died for her sins demanded her liberation.

The words of Christ are wonderful because of their wisdom. He has the answer, my friend. This world today is filled with people who do not have the answer to their needs. I am preaching to someone today who does not have the answer to life's problems. You are like a plane without a pilot, like a ship without a rudder— drifting, seeking, searching, wandering across the face of the earth like a fugitive from justice. You are wondering, *Is there no answer? Is there no message? Is there no one who can tell me how to get out?* Yes, there is: Jesus can. The words of Christ are in season to the weary soul. He has the message all of us need.

There was an old grandmother somewhere in Europe way back in history. The king had died. He had twin sons. Both were to become the rulers of the kingdom, and they were just children. They had no wisdom with which to rule a nation, and the people said, "What shall we do?"

The wise grandmother said, "I raised my son. He was a wonderful king. He knew how to rule, reign and love. Oh, he was a great man. These are his boys. I think I know what to tell them." She said, "Put them upon the throne, and I will sit in back of the throne. When the subjects come to them and ask, 'What shall we do? what is your judgment? what is your discernment? what is your decision?' from behind them I will whisper the answer."

It is said that for years a nation was ruled in that fashion.

Thank God, there is One with every one of us who are saved this morning who has the answer—Jesus!

"It is the spirit that quickeneth; the flesh profiteth nothing: the words that I speak unto you, they are spirit, and they are life."

III. WONDERFUL BECAUSE THEY HAVE SUPERNATURAL POWER

A centurion had a sick servant who was ready to die. He sent a man to Jesus, "beseeching him that he would come and heal his servant." The centurion sent word to the Lord, "Trouble not thyself: for I am not worthy that thou shouldest enter under my roof...but say in a word, and my servant shall be healed." He did not wish to trouble the Master overly. This centurion said, 'I also am a man set under authority...I say unto one, Go, and he goeth; and to another, Come, and he cometh. So, you don't have to go to my house. But *say a word*, and my servant will be healed' (Luke 7).

There is a wonderful lesson here. This man said, "Jesus, if You say it, that is all I need. You don't have to come and touch him physically. Just say a word." So Jesus said a word, and that servant was healed.

At the words of Jesus, everything that exists today came into being.

"In the beginning was the Word, and the Word was with God, and the Word was God. The same was in the beginning with God. All things were made by him; and without him was not any thing made that was made."—John 1:1–3.

He just stepped out on the horizon of eternity in the morning of the beginning and said, "Let there be...," and here it is. The words of Jesus have supernatural power.

We see that at the grave of Lazarus. He stood in that Silent City of the Dead at the tomb of one of His friends who had loved Him and had opened his home to Him. He had been dead for four days. Jesus said, "Lazarus, come forth."

Dwight L. Moody said, "If he hadn't said, '*Lazarus,* come forth,' every dead person in that cemetery would have come out of his grave."

"And when he thus had spoken, he cried with a loud voice, Lazarus, come forth. And he that was dead came forth, bound hand and foot with graveclothes: and his face was bound about with a napkin. Jesus saith unto them, Loose him, and let him go."— John 11:43, 44.

Great forces are meeting: death and decay and putrefaction. A man for four days had been on the other side, in death, wrapped in graveclothes and placed in a tomb. The tomb was sealed. Here was that mighty power against which, humanly speaking, neither you nor I have any power. But there stepped up to that grave the Author of Life. I see, in my imagination, the "David of life" meet the "Goliath of death," and with one word He slays him. Death cries, "I cannot hold him." Jesus says, "Loose him, and let him go." Out of a grave there walks a man, breathing and living and shouting the praises of God.

Oh, the words of Jesus! That is why, with God's help, I would like to be known as a Bible preacher. Nothing in this world is like the supernatural words of Jesus Christ.

IV. WONDERFUL WORDS BECAUSE THEY ARE LIFE-GIVING

Just as physical life was given to Lazarus by the word of Christ, we read that these are life-giving words.

Jesus told a parable of a sower who went forth to sow. He told of a fourfold response you should get from sowing the seed—the hardhearted, the halfhearted, the shallow-hearted and the whole-hearted. Then when Jesus started to explain that parable of the sower sowing the seed, He said, "The sower soweth the word." The seed is the Word of God. There is life in a seed.

I will never forget the first time I was on a farm where corn had been planted. Some of it had been planted long enough for it to come up. Some had just been planted and hadn't come up.

You take a kernel of corn and put it down in the ground. After awhile a little green shoot comes up. It grows into a stalk, and leaves come on it. Then one or more ears come on it. That little piece of corn reproduces itself several hundred times in just a few weeks.

Curiosity got the best of me, and I said to myself, *What is going on down there?* I dug in the dirt until I found a kernel. That little seed had turned black, and putrefaction literally had set in. But out of it came a little green shoot—out of death came life. Out of a seed came more life and new seed. "Verily, verily, I say unto you, Except a corn of wheat fall into the ground and die, it abideth alone: but if it die, it bringeth forth much fruit" (John 12:24).

That is what this Bible is—the Seed, the Word of the eternal, living God. Exodus 16:4 says, "Behold, I will rain bread from heaven for you. . . ." Deuteronomy 8:3 says, ". . . man doth not live by bread only, but by every word that proceedeth out of the mouth of the Lord doth man live." There is life in these words.

Even Jesus quoted it later, saying, "Man shall not live by bread alone, but by every word that proceedeth out of the mouth of God" (Matt. 4:4). There is life in these words.

Everywhere I go people are talking about what is going to happen. They will refer to many great crises that are abroad in the world and in our nation and say, "What in the world is going to happen? Where is it all going to lead?" People's hearts are literally failing them for fear. Yet Jesus said in John 8:51, "If a man keep my saying, he shall never see death." The Christian is going to live forever, for the words of Christ are life-giving.

"...the words that I speak unto you, they are spirit, and they are life."

V. WONDERFUL BECAUSE THEY ARE LIBERATING WORDS

They will set you free. Jesus said, "And ye shall know the truth, and the truth shall make you free."

I often think of the slave days, a tragic thing in our nation. We are reaping the results now and probably will until Jesus comes. Regardless of what you think about it, a human being is not to be sold like an animal. But they were in our nation.

In New Orleans, Louisiana, where I was born years ago, a tall, healthy, wonderfully built black man stood on the block while people bid for his services. As people bid, he would dash against his chains that bound him and rail out at them as they sought to become his owner and master.

One man kept bidding higher and higher. Finally, the bidding closed, and this highest bidder won the man.

The black man strained against the chains and gave out vilifications against him. But the man who bought him walked up, took the key from the auctioneer, unlocked the lock, took it out of the chain and threw it away. He took the chains from his wrists and legs and threw them down on the ground, turned his back and started walking away. He said, "You are now a free man."

The black man, stunned and shocked for a moment, stood and gazed on the back of the departing man; then he ran and fell down at his feet and said, "I want to belong to one like you." The black man followed him home and became his own.

Jesus does that, thank God! He comes into the slave markets of sin, bids the highest price—the price of His spotless, precious blood—saves people and liberates them. The only free people on earth are those who are saved. "And ye shall know the truth, and the truth shall make you free."

VI. WONDERFUL BECAUSE THEY ARE ETERNAL WORDS

"Heaven and earth shall pass away, but my words shall not pass away," says Matthew 24:35. When you drop the seed in one's heart, only God knows what it might do.

I preached in Toronto last Sunday and Monday. Monday night my wife and I were talking to people at the close of the service in the Forward Baptist Church. A fine-looking man came up to me and gripped my hand. Folks were standing all around, but he had something to say that must be said:

> Brother Malone, I have not discussed it with you before, but I must now tell you. Three years ago you spoke in the Jarvis Street Baptist Church here in Toronto. I had been in the ministry for years but had backslidden and had gotten out of the ministry. I had gone back into business. I was a miserable soul.
>
> That night at Jarvis Street Baptist Church I listened to you preach. While others responded, I didn't. But something dropped in my heart that night that I couldn't get over. A few months later, I surrendered my life afresh to God; and I am back in the ministry. My family and I are now happy. My church is growing, and sometime I hope you will come and preach for me.

My wife was standing nearby and I said, "Come here a minute, Honey." She came over and I said, "I want you to tell it over again to her." He did. Afterwards I said, "If nothing else was accomplished in a visit three years ago to the city of Toronto, this one thing was worth it. Something was dropped in a man's heart that got him back on the right path."

VII. WONDERFUL BECAUSE THEY ARE CLEANSING WORDS

Jesus said, "Now ye are clean through the word which I have spoken unto you" (John 15:3). It is like the lepers that came. When He saw them, He said unto them, "Go shew yourselves unto the priests. And it came to pass, that, as they went, they were cleansed" (Luke 17:14)—all by the good Word of God. There is nothing like the Word of God.

The wonderful words of Jesus are spirit, and they are life. They are salvation and forgiveness to all who believe.

Many wonderful things have happened through tracts. There was a man in the United States a few years ago known as a highway evangelist, Henry Goodger. He rode a bicycle thousands of miles all over this country giving out tracts. He would arrive at a place and go door to door. He would talk to people, then leave a tract. Once he rang a doorbell SIX times and waited for a response. Five times no one answered; the sixth time, a man opened the door and roughly said, "What do you want?"

Mr. Goodger said, "I want to give you a message and tell you the most wonderful words you have ever heard. I want to tell you that Christ died for you, and I want to leave this tract with you." The man snatched it out of his hand and slammed the door.

Henry Goodger left. He couldn't get that home off his mind because God was working.

Some days later he went back and rang the doorbell just one time. The man came to the door, meek as a lamb, and said, "Come on in. I want you to follow me up the stairs yonder to the attic." Up the stairs they went. This man said:

You see that rope hanging there with the loop at the end? That

is a hangman's noose. You see that box there? A few days ago
I was standing on it with that noose around my neck. I had nothing to live for. I was literally at the end of my rope. But someone rang the doorbell, once, twice, three times, four times, five
times. I said to myself, *What does it matter? I am ending it all
anyhow.* But the sixth time it rang I lifted the noose from my
neck, stepped down off of the box and said, *I will get rid of
whoever it is, then finish the job.* But you said some words and
left some words in this tract that I can't get over. I am now
a new man.

He sat on the box that he had stood on a few days ago, and
Henry Goodger sat on a chair in an attic while this man con-
firmed his faith in the Lord Jesus Christ through the Word of
God.

"...the words that I speak unto you, they are spirit, and they
are life"—and the sweetest words you will ever hear. I know,
because they are the sweetest ones that I have ever heard. I heard
it when I was nineteen years old on the road of sin and ruin, and
God changed my life.

FIVE MINUTES AFTER I DIE

Loved ones will weep o'er my silent face,
Dear ones will clasp me in sad embrace,
Shadows and darkness will fill the place
    Five minutes after I die.

Faces that sorrow I will not see,
Voices that murmur will not reach me,
But where, oh, where will my soul be
    Five minutes after I die?

Quickly the years of my life have flown,
Gathering treasures I thought my own;
Then I must reap the seeds I have sown
    Five minutes after I die.

Naught to repair the good I lack;
Fixed to the goal of my chosen track,
No room to repent, no turning back,
    Five minutes after I die.

Now I can stifle convictions stirred,
Now I can silence the voice oft heard;
Then the fulfillment of God's sure Word
    Five minutes after I die.

Mated forever with my chosen throng.
Long is eternity, oh, so long!
Then woe is me if my soul be wrong
    Five minutes after I die!

Oh, what a fool—hard the word, but true,
Passing the Saviour with death in view,
Doing a deed I can never undo—
    Five minutes after I die.

Thanks to the Lord Jesus for pardon free;
He paid my debt on Calvary's tree;
Heaven's gates will enfold even me
    Five minutes after I die.

O marvelous grace that has rescued me,
O joyous moment when Jesus I see,
O happy day when with Him I'll be
    Five minutes after I die.

God help you to choose. Your eternal state
Depends on your choice; you dare not wait.
You must choose now: it will be too late
    Five minutes after you die!

                    —Author Unknown

"It is the spirit that quickeneth; the flesh profiteth nothing: the words that I speak unto you, they are spirit, and they are life."—John 6:63.

Chapter IX

Seven Wonders of Hell

(Sermon preached December 15, 1956)

"And whosoever was not found written in the book of life was cast into the lake of fire."—Rev. 20:15.

God said in His Word that His thoughts and ways are as high above man's thoughts and ways as the heavens are above the earth. How true this is in regard to the truth of the eternal punishment of the wicked. It is a stupendous truth which causes me to stand in awe and wonder. I marvel at the statements in the Bible which have to do with the eternal torment of those not saved.

I am not the first, by any means, to marvel at God's truth. This certainly was true of Nicodemus in John 3, who came to Jesus by night and heard Jesus say to him, "Ye must be born again," because, "Except a man be born again, he cannot see the kingdom of God." We read how "Nicodemus saith unto him, How can a man be born when he is old? can he enter the second time into his mother's womb, and be born?" Jesus said, "Marvel not that I said unto thee, Ye must be born again." Evidently Nicodemus marveled and wondered at the truth of God.

This is true also in chapter 5 of John where Jesus told the Jews He was the Son of God and equal with God. He told the Jews how He was able to give life to men and raise people from the dead. They marveled and wondered at such statements. In verses 28 and 29 Jesus said:

"Marvel not at this: for the hour is coming, in the which all that are in the graves shall hear his voice, And shall come forth; they that have done good, unto the resurrection of life; and they that have done evil, unto the resurrection of damnation."

On the Isle of Patmos John also had received the revelation from the Lord Jesus Christ. He had a vision of things that caused him to marvel and wonder. In chapter 17 of Revelation where he was given a vision and a picture of God's wrath and judgment upon the false and apostate religions of the end time, we read how the angels said unto him, "Wherefore didst thou marvel? I will tell thee the mystery of the woman, and of the beast that carrieth her, which hath the seven heads and ten horns."

So God's truth caused men to marvel and wonder and stand in awe at the stupendous statements found in the Word of God. I certainly stand in awe and marvel when it comes to the matter of Hell. It is such an awful fact. Men ought to face it. I pray God that it may dawn upon your heart today that there is a Hell to which sinners go. I am not merely concerned in this message with impressing the fact of Hell upon the hearts and minds of the unsaved. But Christian people around the world need to be constantly reminded that Hell is no myth, no fable, but an awful reality taught throughout the Bible.

It is said that a group of preachers were talking, and Dwight L. Moody was in their midst. One man made a flippant, jesting remark about Hell. Everyone laughed except Mr. Moody. Later a preacher said, "Mr. Moody, I noticed you didn't laugh at the little joke told about Hell. Why?" With a broken heart over lost sinners and tears coming to his eyes, Mr. Moody looked at the man and said, "My friend, Hell is no joke."

How true, dear friend. Hell is no joke. Hell is an awful reality.

May God help both saved and unsaved to face its reality.

I. ITS EXISTENCE

Hell is a fact, an awful reality, and is taught throughout God's Book. In Matthew 23:33 Jesus said, "Ye serpents, ye generation of vipers, how can ye escape the damnation of hell?" Notice in the Gospels how much Jesus talked about Hell. In chapter 9 of Mark, verse 43, He uses some of the strongest language in referring to Hell:

"And if thy hand offend thee, cut it off: it is better for thee to enter into life maimed, than having two hands to go into hell, into the fire that never shall be quenched: Where their worm dieth not, and the fire is not quenched."

He also said,

"If thy foot offend thee, cut it off: it is better for thee to enter halt into life, than having two feet to be cast into hell, into the fire that never shall be quenched: Where their worm dieth not, and the fire is not quenched."

In speaking of Hell, Jesus thought it was such a terrible place that it would be better to be blind in this life than to have two good eyes and stumble into Hell. He taught it would be better to be without one's limbs and be crippled and halt and maimed in this life than to be lost in sin and go to Hell and perish, forever separated from God.

Some time ago I stood by the bedside of a young man who had lost one of his legs in a shooting accident. I asked him if he were a Christian.

He said, "Yes, Brother Malone, I'm saved. I'm a child of God."

"When were you saved?"

"Here on this bed. I was in such awful pain for four hours, and I knew I couldn't stand it any longer, so I called on God to help me and to save me. I know that He saved me, and I am now a Christian." Then he added, "This accident happened for a reason. As a result of losing my leg, I have gotten my soul saved. I'd rather have one leg and be saved than to have two legs and die in sin and go to Hell."

I say the same thing. I'd rather lose both eyes, both hands, both legs and be saved and have a new body, incorruptible and undefiled in Heaven and be with the Lord Jesus forever, than to go through life with the best of health and be lost forever.

Jesus spoke of Hell in chapter 16 of Luke. He told of a rich man who died, "And in hell he lift up his eyes, being in torments, and seeth Abraham afar off, and Lazarus in his bosom."

You want to remember that Jesus spoke of the wrath of God and the judgment of God upon sin and against sinners. It was Jesus who said in John 3:36, "He that believeth on the Son hath everlasting life: and he that believeth not the Son shall not see life; but the wrath of God abideth on him." Yes, throughout God's Word we are taught the reality and existence of Hell.

We read in Psalm 9:17, "The wicked shall be turned into hell, and all the nations that forget God." And in Revelation 14:11 we read, "And the smoke of their torment ascendeth up for ever and ever: and they have no rest day nor night, who worship the beast. . . ."

And in II Thessalonians 1:8 Paul writes of the Lord Jesus coming "in flaming fire taking vengeance on them that know not God, and that obey not the gospel of our Lord Jesus Christ: Who shall be punished with everlasting destruction from the presence of the Lord, and from the glory of his power."

James 3:6 speaks of the tongue's being "set on fire of hell."

In Jude, verse 7, the writer refers to the destruction of Sodom and Gomorrah as being "set forth for an example, suffering the vengeance of eternal fire." In verse 13 he speaks of the lost as being "wandering stars, to whom is reserved the blackness of darkness for ever."

False religions and false cults abroad in the land today teach there is no Hell. But God's Word says there is.

"And whosoever was not found written in the book of life was cast into the lake of fire."

II. HELL'S INHABITANTS

Revelation 21:8 tells of Hell's population or the inhabitants or the citizens of Hell:

"But the fearful, and unbelieving, and the abominable, and murderers, and whoremongers, and sorcerers, and idolators, and all liars, shall have their part in the lake which burneth with fire and brimstone: which is the second death."

There are eight classes of people, starting with the fearful or cowardly, and ending up with the liars, all of whom will have their part in the lake of fire. God gives us the record of what kind of people will be in Hell. Of course, no Christian will be there. There will be no Bible there, no churches there, no Gospel there, no singing there, no Holy Spirit there.

One night while the bombing was going on in the city of London and buildings were being destroyed and lives were being snuffed out, a man cried in the midst of his suffering, "This is Hell!"

Another stepped up to him and said, "No, this is not Hell."

The first man said, "How do you know this is not Hell?"

The answer he heard was, "Because there are Christians in this section, and no Christians will be in Hell." He added, "The Salvation Army workers are around the corner yonder preaching the Gospel even now; and there's no Gospel in Hell." He continued: "I'm a Christian, and I love the Lord, and I know I'm not in Hell and never will be."

J. Wilbur Chapman tells of an unsaved girl who had a Christian father. Upon one occasion, the two were riding the train together. The father stepped into another section of the train;

then the girl became surrounded by young men taking God's name in vain and using all sorts of vulgarity. It shocked her to hear what they had to say, to hear them blaspheme the name of God.

When her father returned to the coach, she said, "Father, let's get out of here immediately." They went into another car and sat down. The girl leaned her head on her father's shoulder and began to weep. "Oh, Father, how vulgar and profane they were! I couldn't stand it another minute."

The father said, "Daughter, do you realize that is the kind of people who are going to Hell? You're unsaved and on your way to Hell, too. And that is the kind of people you're going to spend eternity with."

She said, "Oh, Father, tell me how to be saved once more; then I will trust the Lord. I don't want to be in Hell with that kind of people."

Thank God, I'm going to spend eternity in Heaven with the saints of all the ages and not in Hell with such a crowd as is described in Revelation 21:8!

Every coward in all the world will be there. A young man recently said to me, "Mr. Malone, I suppose you have heard every excuse in the world for people not being saved, but I am going to be honest with you. The reason I'm not a Christian is I'm too big a coward. I'm afraid to walk down that aisle and then hear the laughing and sneering of my unsaved friends who will make fun of me if I trust the Lord. I'm too big a coward."

Yes, the cowards will be in Hell. This verse says the fearful and unbelieving will be there.

III. HELL'S LACK OF FELLOWSHIP

There's no fellowship in Hell. The Bible speaks of it as a place where there is weeping and wailing and gnashing of teeth.

In Luke 16 Jesus told of a rich man who went to Hell. He lifted up his eyes, being in torment, and begged for water. He asked

Abraham to send someone to his father's house, for he had five brothers unsaved and he wanted them to be warned that Hell is an awful fact. Here are his exact words: "I pray thee therefore, father, that thou wouldest send him to my father's house: For I have five brethren; that he may testify unto them, lest they also come into this place of torment." This rich man didn't want his brothers to come where he was. They would have been no comfort to him, for there is no fellowship in Hell.

Some years ago I had a peculiar experience. A young man raised his hand two or three times at Emmanuel Baptist Church, requesting prayer; but he would make no decision for Christ. Seeing the troubled look on his face, I finally went back to the door before he could get away and spoke to him. I asked him why he wouldn't be saved. He said, "Mr. Malone, I'll tell you why. My wife died at the age of twenty. When we were married she said to me, 'Pete, we ought to go to church, give our lives to the Lord and have a Christian home.' I said to her, 'Not for awhile. We will first have some fun, enjoy life; then when we are older, we'll settle down and give our hearts to the Lord.'

"Then one night after we had been to a dance, warm and perspiring, we went out into the cool night air. My wife took pneumonia and in a few days died and went out to meet God unsaved. I kept her from being saved. I wouldn't let her trust the Lord. My wife is now in Hell! If you think I'm going to trust Jesus and go up yonder to be with the Lord when my wife is in Hell, Preacher, you've got another thought coming." He walked out of the door very hurriedly, and I've never seen him since.

How I wanted to tell that young man that if his wife could talk to him, she would beg him not to come there. If his wife could speak to him, she would plead with him to be saved, for he will be no consolation to her and she will be none to him in Hell. There is no fellowship in Hell.

"And whosoever was not found written in the book of life was cast into the lake of fire."

IV. HELL'S PUNISHMENT

The punishment of Hell will be more than the punishment of flames and fervent heat. There are two significant things about Hell that the Bible teaches will be unbearable. First, being forsaken of God. When Jesus died on the cross, He cried, "My God, my God, why hast thou forsaken me?" There, taking the sinner's place, He was for awhile forsaken by God. When He cried, God didn't answer Him. God turned His back on His Son. He turned His face away as Christ became a sin-offering for us. That is a picture of the sinner lost and in Hell, forsaken by God.

Second Thessalonians 1:9 speaks of being punished with everlasting destruction from the presence of the Lord and from the glory of His power. Some translators have said this word "destruction" means everlasting seclusion, or expulsion, from the presence of the Lord. It is an everlasting punishment, so it cannot be annihilation, as some would have us believe. Annihilation is momentary; this punishment is everlasting. It never ends.

The second awful thing about Hell will be one's memory. In Luke 16 Abraham is quoted as saying to the lost man in Hell, "Son, remember that thou in thy lifetime receivedst thy good things." Yes, you had your chances, your opportunities, but you wouldn't be saved. Now remember it. And remember it forever. While the ages roll on, while the fires of Hell burn and never go out—remember. Remember, you had your chance to be saved. Remember every song you ever heard, every prayer that was ever prayed, every sermon that was ever preached—remember! Remember the people who tried to get you to be a Christian. Remember those who loved you, pleaded with you, and prayed for you. Remember! Remember your sins. Remember how you influenced others, damned the souls of others, and sent them to Hell.

Memory! Memory! Oh, its awful pains and torments in Hell! Memory will make Hell an awful place.

V. HELL HAS NO EXIT

Noah's ark was sealed by God Himself. No one could get in, and no one could get out. God had shut the door, and no man could open it. How true of Hell! God will seal it up.

The picture in chapter 20 of Revelation is of Satan being cast into the bottomless pit by a strong angel who

"Cast him into the bottomless pit, and shut him up, and set a seal upon him, that he should deceive the nations no more, till the thousand years should be fulfilled: and after that he must be loosed a little season."

Now when God closes and seals something, it is closed forever. Hell has no exit. There is no arrow pointing, **THIS WAY OUT.** There is no red light over a door, **EXIT.** There is no fire escape, no door that swings out.

I recently read of the coal miners who lost their lives while being sealed up a mile and a half below the earth. An awful tragedy! An awful fate!

But think of it, friend, the sinner is in Hell forever, without one ray of light, not one bit of hope, with no windows, no doors, no exit. Sealed forever by the power of God, separated from God's face in torment and punishment forever and ever!

"And whosoever was not found written in the book of life was cast into the lake of fire."

VI. HELL HAS NO END

Hell will never end. If I know my heart, I have studied the Word of God with an unbiased mind. I want to learn what it teaches on Hell as well as on all other subjects. The Bible teaches that Hell is everlasting. "The smoke of their torment ascendeth up for ever and ever." We read of eternal fire and eternal punishment. Now "eternal" is used in relation to the bliss of the eternal home of the saved. If Hell is not eternal, neither is the spiritual life that has been imparted unto us which is called everlasting life. The Greek word for "eternal, everlasting" means "age upon age without end."

This is God's picture, God's description of Hell. It has no end. It will never come to an end.

In Revelation 22:11 God says, "He that is unjust, let him be unjust still: and he which is filthy, let him be filthy still: and he that is righteous, let him be righteous still: and he that is holy, let him be holy still."

You go into Hell unsaved—then that's the way it will forever be. You go there filthy, unrighteous, lost—that's the way it will be forever, world without end.

Some years ago I visited a man in Greenville, South Carolina. I think he was the most pitiful human being I had ever seen. He had been bedfast for ten years, paralyzed with arthritis and absolutely helpless. He was stone blind. His eyes were literally petrified in his head. He was fed by the kind hands of loved ones. He could barely speak. He couldn't move a hand or a limb. He was more dead than alive. Yet he was a wonderful Christian.

When I saw him, my heart broke. I thanked God for my health and His goodness to me. I bent over his bed and said, "Dear friend, I'm sorry you're so sick. My heart goes out to you. I've come to pray for you." Through his almost clenched teeth, he said to me, "Friend, I won't be this way forever. Since I'm a Christian, I'm going to be well someday when the Lord gives me my resurrection body." Then he added, with much effort, "The ones I pity are those who are lost and going to Hell to suffer forever." Yes, Hell has no end.

VII. PEOPLE CONTINUE TO GO THERE

In Matthew 25:41 we read where Jesus, on the occasion of the judgment of the nations, will say unto those on the left hand, "Depart from me, ye cursed, into everlasting fire, prepared for the devil and his angels."

Hell has been prepared for the Devil and his angels. But it is a mystery that people will continue to reject Christ, refuse to accept His free offer of full pardon and salvation and continue on that downward, broad road that leads to Hell. Yes, I'm amazed that folks refuse God's offering, turn down God's mercy, and go on their way, rejecting Christ, knowing that it leads to Hell.

A skeptic once asked a humble Christian, "Where is Hell?" The Christian replied, "At the end of a Christless life." At the end of a Christless life is an eternal Hell, according to God's Word. The only thing between you and Hell is one heartbeat. To those unsaved I warn: if your heart should miss a beat, if it should cease to beat one time, then you would be lost forever. May God help you to think on your way and to trust Him today.

When I was a student at Bob Jones University, I had a wonderful opportunity to hear Dr. William Edward Beiderwolf, a truly great preacher and soul winner. He held great meetings across America for many years, winning thousands to Christ. I heard Dr. Beiderwolf tell a most touching and sympathetic story of a man and his wife and their grown son who lived together.

One day the wife died and went out to meet God. The father and son, with broken hearts, took her out to the cemetery and laid her away. That night, after the funeral that afternoon, in the home together, the father said to the son, "This will be the most lonely night of my life. See that empty chair sitting across the room in front of the fireplace? There your mother and I have sat together all these years every evening. Will you sit there tonight and take her place? My heart is broken, and I am so lonely." The son said, "No, Dad. I'm going out tonight." The father pleaded and begged—but in vain.

The son went up to his room to prepare to go out and leave his father alone. Dr. Beiderwolf said the father threw himself prostrate across the door. When the son came down, the sight of his father lying across the door so enraged him that he kicked him and stepped over his body, then went out into the night. In the wee hours of the morning, he returned and found his father dead.

You wonder how one could be so cruel and show such ingratitude. Dear friend, if you go to Hell, you step over the crucified body of Christ.

"And whosoever was not found written in the book of life was cast into the lake of fire."—Rev. 20:15.

Chapter X

Multitudes...Judgment-Bound— Hell-Determined

(Preached June 15, 1959)

"But whereunto shall I liken this generation?"—Matt. 11:16.

That question fell from the lips of the lovely Lord Jesus. Jesus had been talking about a great preacher, John the Baptist, now in prison. John the Baptist had thundered forth the message of God without compromise. As he preached on this occasion, he told a man and woman they had no right to live in their sins. He was put in jail as a result of it. While he was in prison, he heard of the mighty works of Jesus—how the blind were made to see, the lame made to walk, the deaf made to hear, the dumb made to speak. He heard how the dead were raised and the sick were made whole. While in prison, John sent a messenger to Jesus to ask this question, "Art thou he that should come, or do we look for another?"

Jesus said, 'Go back and tell John again that the lame leap for joy, the blind see, the deaf hear, the dumb speak and the poor have the Gospel preached to them. That will be the answer that will prove I am He of whom all the Old Testament prophets and preachers prophesied.'

After Jesus had sent the message back to John, He began to speak of John. He said some things about this great preacher that I do not think are said about any other preacher in the Bible. He said John was "more than a prophet." He reminded these people that John was a preacher so important in the plan and program and work of God that his ministry was prophesied in the Old Testament.

Jesus reminded them that the Old Testament recorded how John would come and be His forerunner.

Jesus not only said that John was more than a prophet and that his coming was prophesied in the Old Testament but also that of those born of woman there had not risen a greater than John the Baptist, a man clothed with camel skins who preached the message of repentance and baptized people by the thousands.

After saying that John was the greatest prophet born of woman, Jesus looked around and saw the great multitudes to whom John had been preaching and said, "Whereunto shall I liken this generation?"—a generation to whom John had been preaching for several years. In spite of the preaching of John the Baptist, this greatest of preachers, many had not listened, many would not hear, and thousands were still lost. Many religious people did not get right.

This text, "Whereunto shall I liken this generation?" among other things, has reference to the ministry of John the Baptist. He lived right, he preached the Truth, but he couldn't win everybody. Multitudes were still on their way to Hell. Multitudes were judgment-bound and Hell-determined, in spite of the great ministry of a great preacher.

I want us to notice five things in the Gospels that Jesus said about His generation. Those same things that Jesus said about the generation in which He lived for thirty-three years, I could say about mine, the one in which I have lived for forty-three years. People have not changed. Human nature is the same today as it was when God formed man out of the dust of the ground and when man disobeyed and fell in the Edenic paradise. Man without God will be the same until the day Jesus blows His trumpet and comes to receive the church. Human nature never changes. Anything that Jesus said about His generation is true of my generation. The Son of God takes divine x-rays of human nature and interprets to us the tragic realities.

I. AN INDIFFERENT GENERATION

First, Jesus taught that His was an indifferent generation.

"But whereunto shall I liken this generation? It is like unto children sitting in the markets, and calling unto their fellows, And saying, We have piped unto you, and ye have not danced; we have mourned unto you, and ye have not lamented."—Matt. 11:16, 17.

Jesus said, 'I liken this generation unto a group of children playing in the street.' Children are imitators. They imitate people and things. Jesus said these children are imitating two things: a dance and a funeral. First, they say, "We have piped unto you." They blew their little horns and made their little music, but nobody responded and nobody came to play. Jesus said this is the way multitudes are. "We have piped unto you, and ye have not danced."

Then the little children imitate a funeral. They say, "We have mourned unto you, and ye have not lamented." In other words, "Somebody is dead. We are mourning; our hearts are broken, but you have not lamented with us, and you have not wept with us."

Jesus said that is the way this generation is. It is an indifferent generation. "We have piped unto you, and ye have not danced; we have mourned unto you, and ye have not lamented."

In spite of folks being saved and in spite of the evidence of the blessing of God, the spirit of revival and the work of the Lord in the hearts of multitudes, there has never been a generation more indifferent to the Gospel than this one. I did not say indifferent to religion but indifferent to the Gospel.

I went into a home where an unsaved man was not going to live long. He was propped up in a chair. His hands were trembling. This was the second time I had been there to try to talk to him about his soul. His wife, son and son-in-law were sitting in the living room with him. They knew he was going to die. I sat down beside him and began talking about his soul. The television was going; a cowboy picture was on with guns ablazing and horses running. Those people were not even interested enough to turn the television off.

I asked the sick and dying man if he knew he was going to leave this world pretty soon.

"Yes, I know it, Mr. Malone."

"Would you like to be a Christian?" I asked.

He replied, "Well, I ought to be, but I feel I've waited too late; I've gone too far; I've put it off too long."

The television was still going. His son-in-law and wife were still watching it. What did they care about his soul? They knew he was going to Hell, but they were not even interested enough to shut off a television with a cowboy picture. Were those people interested in a man's soul? No! I say, this is an indifferent generation.

One week exactly from that night when I pleaded with that man to be saved, he died without hope and without God and is now in Hell as far as I know. When the news came of his death, I couldn't help but think how different it might have been. Suppose his grown children had shut off the television and come in tears and said, "Daddy, please be saved; you are soon to meet God, and you are yet in your sins." No doubt he would have been saved.

Suppose he had said, "Mr. Malone, I am at the end of the journey, and I have lived without God until this solemn hour. Please tell me how I can be forgiven of my sins and be saved from Hell and judgment." He would have been rejoicing in Heaven today with the angels of God instead of suffering in Hell with the lost of all ages.

O Indifference—how many you have slain! How many you have sent to a Christless grave and an eternal Hell! O Indifference— how many you have held in your captivity until their doom was sealed forever!

Indifference speaks of a heart which is being hardened against God. God's Word says:

"*Wherefore (as the Holy Ghost saith, To day if ye will hear his*

*voice, Harden not your hearts, as in the provocation, in the day
of temptation in the wilderness: When your fathers tempted me,
proved me, and saw my works forty years. Wherefore I was grieved
with that generation, and said, They do always err in their heart;
and they have not known my ways. So I sware in my wrath, They
shall not enter into my rest.)''*—Heb. 3:7-11.

''Whereunto shall I liken this generation?''

II. A RELIGIOUS-BUT-LOST GENERATION

Jesus taught that His was a religious-but-lost generation. Now
notice something in Matthew 3:7, 8:

''But when he [John the Baptist] *saw many of the Pharisees and
Sadducees come to his baptism, he said unto them, O generation
of vipers, who hath warned you to flee from the wrath to come?
Bring forth therefore fruits meet for repentance.''*

Here is what happened. John was out preaching repentance:
'Unless you repent, you are not going to be saved.' He said,
'Repent or perish.'

Listen! There is no such thing as being saved in your sins. You
must repent according to the Bible. Some folks were coming, hearing, believing, repenting and being baptized.

The Sadducees came. They said, ''We want to be baptized; we
want to join with you.'' Who were the Sadducees? People who did
not believe in miracles, who did not believe in angels, who did
not believe in the resurrection. They said, ''John, we want you
to baptize us.''

John said, ''I won't baptize you. You Sadducees must bring forth
fruit meet for repentance. You repent like anybody else. You get
right with God. You believe and cast aside your old, dead, formal, ritualistic religion; then I'll baptize you.''

The orthodox Pharisees came. They said, ''We believe the
Bible.'' (They had 600 prohibitions, 600 things they said not to

do. They wore long robes and went to the Temple every day.) They came out to John and said, "Baptize me."

John said, "I won't do it. If I did I would put you down a lost sinner and bring you up a lost sinner. You have religion, but you are lost."

It was a religious generation.

That is true of the generation in which we are living. I read a paragraph of a personal letter I recently received from someone I do not know. The letter begins:

> Dear Sir:
>
>   This is a story that is almost unbelievable, yet it is true. I'm writing you as my last hope. I was baptized and joined a fundamental church without being born again, even though I said I was. For fifteen years I've lived the life of a Christian. I've been very active, even teaching Sunday school. I love the church and all of God's people. Now, suddenly, I realize what I've done and know that the only end of this is Hell. Is there any chance now that God will forgive me and save me?

That is the first paragraph of a letter I received from a woman who joined the church and was baptized fifteen years ago. She is religious but lost. She has been teaching a Sunday school class. For fifteen years she has been just as religious as anybody else but writes, "I was baptized and joined the church without being born again." Now after fifteen years she asks, "Is there any hope for me? The only end of this is Hell."

Jesus' generation was a religious—but lost—generation. So is this twentieth-century generation.

I have seen on television and read in newspapers the accounts of great so-called revival campaigns in our day where thousands professed to be saved. I've talked to some preachers in cities where these campaigns have been conducted. Not one has had one person join his church, not one has had one person attend prayer meeting at his church, not a person has started tithing as a result of the so-called revival campaign.

That is not of God, and I want no part of it. One thing wrong today is that the line of separation has been broken down. God never told a preacher to associate with a blatant infidel. God never told a preacher to associate with people who don't believe in the virgin birth, in the bodily resurrection, in the literal second coming of Jesus.

The last time I attended a ministerial association meeting, I heard a discussion as to whether a man could be a Christian and not believe in the virgin birth. The ministers in the association were divided. Part of them said, "You can be a Christian and not believe in the virgin birth." I told myself I would never go to another ministerial association of that kind. And I haven't been to one since. And that's not all—I'm not going to. I'm not going to rub shoulders with somebody who believes Jesus Christ was an illegitimate child. The Bible says if such a one comes to your house, don't open the door and let him in. God expects preachers and churches to be separated in the things of the Word of God.

Religious Pharisees and Sadducees came out and said, "We want to join you. We want to get baptized." The Bible describes many of this generation as "having a form of godliness, but denying the power thereof: from such turn away" (II Tim. 3:5).

Jesus spoke of this tragic matter also when He said:

"Not every one that saith unto me, Lord, Lord, shall enter into the kingdom of heaven; but he that doeth the will of my Father which is in heaven. Many will say to me in that day, Lord, Lord, have we not prophesied in thy name? and in thy name have cast out devils? and in thy name done many wonderful works? And then will I profess unto them, I never knew you: depart from me, ye that work iniquity."—Matt. 7:21–23.

Again He spoke of it when He said, "Except your righteousness shall exceed the righteousness of the scribes and Pharisees, ye shall in no case enter into the kingdom of heaven" (Matt. 5:20).

Remember that Nicodemus of John 3 was religious but lost; and to him Jesus said, "Except a man be born again, he cannot see the kingdom of God" and "Marvel not that I said unto thee, Ye must be born again."

III. AN EVIL GENERATION

Jesus taught that His was an evil generation: "O generation of vipers, how can ye, being evil, speak good things? for out of the abundance of the heart the mouth speaketh" (Matt. 12:34); "An evil and adulterous generation. . ." (Matt. 12:39); "this wicked generation" (Matt. 12:45); "O faithless and perverse generation, how long shall I be with you?" (Matt. 17:17).

Ours, too, is a wicked generation. There is wickedness in high places, wickedness in politics, wickedness in so-called churches and religious organizations. God have mercy!

"Whereunto shall I liken this generation?" Much emphasis is given in the Bible to the wickedness and depravity of man. This was true in Noah's day, for we read, "And God saw that the wickedness of man was great in the earth, and that every imagination of the thoughts of his heart was only evil continually" (Gen. 6:5). This was true when God destroyed the cities of Sodom and Gomorrah. Of their wickedness, God spoke, saying, "Because the cry of Sodom and Gomorrah is great, and because their sin is very grievous. . ." (Gen. 18:20). God has always taken note of wicked men, wicked nations, wicked cities. He saw the wickedness of Nineveh and said to Jonah, "Arise, go to Nineveh, that great city, and cry against it; for their wickedness is come up before me" (Jonah 1:2).

The Bible says man is depraved, degenerate and lost. The Bible says, "The heart is deceitful above all things, and desperately wicked: who can know it?" (Jer. 17:9); "All we like sheep have gone astray; we have turned every one to his own way; and the Lord hath laid on him the iniquity of us all" (Isa. 53:6); "For all have sinned, and come short of the glory of God" (Rom. 3:23).

The Bible describes man as he really is. It takes all of the veneer away from the heart. The Bible opens up the human soul like taking the top off a casket and shows it full of dead men's bones and every kind of sin that it is possible for human nature to commit. It teaches that "there is none righteous, no, not one." It teaches that every man, rich or poor, white or black, learned or unlearned, is born in sin and conceived in iniquity and that he will go to Hell not because of what he does but because of what he is, for all men are sinners.

A missionary in Japan said, "These Japanese people are different. They are hard to convince that they need a Saviour." This missionary was talking to a Japanese lady who was educated (95% of them are). This refined, educated Japanese lady said to the missionary who was talking to her about the fact that all have sinned and come short of the glory of God and therefore need a Saviour, "What a ridiculous thought—that I have a corrupt heart, a corrupt nature and need to be born again!"

The missionary said Japanese people are different. I say they are not.

The average person in America laughs at the thought that he is a subject for Hell and the wrath and condemnation of God. But according to God's Word, he is. Every man and woman who does not experience the new birth will suffer in Hell the wrath of an angry God. If the Bible is true, then "ye must be born again."

"Whereunto shall I liken this generation?" It is an evil generation.

IV. A HELL-BOUND GENERATION

Jesus taught that His generation was Hell-bound. Read Matthew 23:33: "Ye serpents, ye generation of vipers, how can ye escape the damnation of hell?" Jesus said His generation was Hell-bound, and so is ours.

"Whereunto shall I liken this generation?" It is a Hell-bound generation. Jesus warned that many are on their way to Hell. He said, "Enter ye in at the strait gate: for wide is the gate, and broad is the way, that leadeth to destruction, and many there be which go in thereat'' (Matt. 7:13). Jesus says that many are lost while few are saved.

Hell is a fact, an awful and terrible reality. Jesus had much to say about Hell. In Mark 9:43–47 He used some of the strongest language in referring to Hell that He ever used on any subject:

"And if thy hand offend thee, cut it off: it is better for thee to enter into life maimed, than having two hands to go into hell, into the fire that never shall be quenched: Where their worm dieth not, and the fire is not quenched. And if thy foot offend thee, cut it off: it is better for thee to enter halt into life, than having two feet to be cast into hell, into the fire that never shall be quenched: Where their worm dieth not, and the fire is not quenched. And if thine eye offend thee, pluck it out: it is better for thee to enter into the kingdom of God with one eye, than having two eyes to be cast into hell fire.''

Jesus warned that Hell is such a terrible place that a man or woman might better lose an eye or a hand or a foot than to stumble into it.

Some time ago I stood by the bedside of a young man who had lost one of his legs in a shooting accident. I asked him, ''Are you a Christian?''

He looked at me and said, ''Yes, Brother Malone, I am saved.''

''When were you saved?'' I asked.

''Here on this bed. I was in such awful pain for four hours, I knew I could stand it no longer. So I called on God to help me, and I asked Him to save me. I know He did. This accident happened for a reason. As a result of losing my leg, I have gotten my soul saved. I would rather have one leg and be saved than have two legs and die in sin and go to Hell.''

I say the same thing. I would rather lose both eyes, both hands, both legs and be saved and have a new body incorruptible and undefiled in Heaven and be with the Lord Jesus forever than to go through life with the best of health and be lost forever.

Jesus spoke of Hell in Luke 16. There He told of a rich man who died and in Hell lifted up his eyes, being in torment.

You want to remember, friend, that Jesus spoke of the wrath and judgment of God upon sin and against sinners. It was Jesus who said, "He that believeth on the Son hath everlasting life; and he that believeth not the Son shall not see life; but the wrath of God abideth on him." Yes, all through the Bible we are warned concerning the reality and existence of Hell.

In Psalm 9:17 we read, "The wicked shall be turned into hell, and all the nations that forget God." We read in Revelation 14:11, "And the smoke of their torment ascendeth up for ever and ever: and they have no rest day nor night, who worship the beast." In II Thessalonians 1:8, Paul writes of the Lord Jesus' coming, "...in flaming fire taking vengeance on them that know not God, and that obey not the gospel of our Lord Jesus Christ: Who shall be punished with everlasting destruction from the presence of the Lord, and from the glory of his power." James 3:6 speaks of the tongue's being set on fire of Hell. In Jude, verse 7, the writer refers to the destruction of Sodom and Gomorrah as being set forth for an example of the suffering and the vengeance of eternal fire. And again, in verse 13, he speaks of the lost as being "wandering stars, to whom is reserved the blackness of darkness for ever."

False religions and false cults abroad in the land today teach there is no Hell, but God's Word teaches there is.

I think the punishment of Hell will be more than the punishment of flames and fervent heat. There are two things about Hell that the Bible teaches will be unbearable:

First, being *forsaken of God*. When Jesus died on the cross, He cried, "My God, my God, why hast thou forsaken me?" He was forsaken of God while taking the sinner's place. God wouldn't listen to Him. God didn't answer Him but turned His back on Him, turned His face away as His Son became a sin-offering for us.

This is a picture of the sinner in Hell, forsaken of God.

The second awful thing about Hell will be *memory*. In Luke 16 Abraham is quoted as saying to the lost man in Hell, "Son, remember." Remember in your lifetime you had your good things. You had your chances, your opportunities; but you wouldn't be saved. Now remember it and remember it forever. While the ages roll on, while the fires of Hell burn and never go out, while age upon age upon age goes across the eternal halls, remember! Remember you had your chance to be saved. Remember every song you heard, every prayer that was prayed, every sermon that was preached. Remember the people who tried to get you to be a Christian. Remember those who loved you and pleaded with you and prayed for you. Remember your sins. Remember how you influenced others, damned their souls and sent them to Hell.

Memory! Memory! Its awful pains and torments will make Hell a terrible place.

V. A JUDGMENT-BOUND GENERATION

Jesus said His generation was a judgment-bound generation. "The men of Nineveh shall rise in judgment with this generation, and shall condemn it: because they repented at the preaching of Jonas; and, behold, a greater than Jonas is here" (Matt. 12:41).

Jesus said that on the day of judgment the men of Nineveh, who repented at the preaching of Jonas, will rise up and condemn the generation of Jesus because they didn't repent at the preaching of John the Baptist and Christ. I wonder who all will rise up in the judgment and condemn our generation, which has heard more preaching than any other generation, yet so many have not yet believed.

If you will not face your sins here and settle up with God, then you must face them at the judgment bar of God. If the Bible be true—and I stake my soul on it—you must bow the knee to Jesus here or hereafter. God's judgment fell often in Old Testament days. History proves that God is a God of wrath and judgment. Hear the Word of God on this matter:

"And the times of this ignorance God winked at; but now commandeth all men every where to repent: Because he hath appointed a day, in the which he will judge the world in righteousness by that man whom he hath ordained; whereof he hath given assurance unto all men, in that he hath raised him from the dead."—Acts 17:30, 31.

God has appointed a day, and Jesus will be the Judge. No one will escape; "every one of us shall give account of himself to God." God is keeping an accurate record, and He knows the names of both the saved and the lost.

"And I saw a great white throne, and him that sat on it, from whose face the earth and the heaven fled away; and there was found no place for them. And I saw the dead, small and great, stand before God; and the books were opened: and another book was opened, which is the book of life: and the dead were judged out of those things which were written in the books, according to their works. And the sea gave up the dead which were in it; and death and hell delivered up the dead which were in them: and they were judged every man according to their works. And death and hell were cast into the lake of fire. This is the second death. And whosoever was not found written in the book of life was cast into the lake of fire."—Rev. 20:11–15.

"Whereunto shall I liken this generation?" It is a judgment-bound generation.

VI. YOU CAN BE SAVED FROM THIS GENERATION

The Bible says you can be saved from this generation. Peter said on the day of Pentecost, "Save yourselves from this untoward [crooked] generation" (Acts 2:40). Though many are deceived, blinded, lost, and undone, they can be saved! The Bible teaches that "whosoever shall call upon the name of the Lord shall be saved" (Rom. 10:13).

This is your golden hour! God is dealing with you, speaking with you. He is knocking at the door of your heart this moment. "Behold, I stand at the door, and knock: if any man hear my voice, and open the door, I will come in to him, and will sup with him, and he with me" (Rev. 3:20). He refuses no one but receives all, declares John 6:37: "All that the Father giveth me shall come to me; and him that cometh to me I will in no wise cast out."

It is said that a captain of a fishing boat prepared to go out to sea. The clouds looked a little dark and treacherous, but he said, "I'm going anyway."

His little fourteen-year-old daughter said, "Daddy, let me go with you today." He didn't want her to go, but she begged, "I'd rather be with you at sea than to be here at home alone." (The mother was dead.)

The captain was afraid of a storm, but his daughter persuaded him.

They got in the boat and sailed to sea. A storm arose. The boat began to toss here and there. Great avalanches of water fell from the sky. The winds blew fiercely.

The captain said to his crew, "We are going to go down." He led his daughter to the mast which had broken off, took some ropes; and while the wind nearly blew them from the deck and the waves dashed across the vessel, he tied the child to the broken mast.

Soon every man was swept overboard, including the father. The ship was torn into dozens of pieces.

When the storm had quieted and the sun was beginning to shine again and the winds had ceased to blow, there floated up to the shore a girl lashed to a piece of wood. She had been saved out of the storm.

The storms of God's judgment are bound to come on this wicked generation. Only those who have by faith lashed their hearts and souls to the truth of the eternal Word and have anchored their souls in the haven of rest will be saved in that day.

"But whereunto shall I liken this generation?"—Matt. 11:16.

Chapter XI

The Forgiveness of Sins

I doubt if I will ever take a shorter text than this one. It has only four words, words which fell from the lips of the Son of God:

"Thy sins are forgiven."—Luke 7:48.

Think about all that is implied in this statement Jesus made to the woman: "Thy sins are forgiven."

The word "forgive," as with its derivatives, "forgiven," "forgiving" or "forgiveness," has a twofold meaning in the Bible. For one thing it means "to cover." Another definition is "a sending away" or a loosing or letting go. In other words, forgiveness is to separate the sinner from his sin and the guilt thereof.

How can that come about? How can any sinner be forgiven? "Thy sins are forgiven," Jesus said. How can that possibly be?

Three preliminary statements come to mind. First, it is impossible to be happy without the knowledge of sins forgiven. "Blessed is he whose transgression is forgiven, whose sin is covered," reads Psalm 32:1. The words "blessed" and "happy" in the Bible are synonymous. It says here, "Happy is he whose sins are forgiven." According to the Bible, there is no such thing as happiness unless we have the knowledge of sins forgiven.

Second, it is possible to have this knowledge. We read in Acts 13:38, "Be it known unto you therefore, men and brethren, that through this man [Jesus] is preached unto you the forgiveness of sins'' through Jesus Christ.

Third, the believers in the New Testament had that knowledge of sins forgiven. They talked about it and never doubted that their past, present and future sins were forgiven. I say that because some people do not believe that you can know beyond any shadow of doubt that all your sins have been eternally and divinely forgiven.

What does the Bible say? Ephesians 1:7 and Colossians 1:14 are identical except for one expression. Colossians 1:14 says, ''In whom we have redemption through his blood, even the forgiveness of sins.'' Ephesians 1:7 reads, ''In whom we have redemption through his blood, the forgiveness of sins, according to the riches of his grace.''

In writing to these two churches, Paul said, 'We have in Him and through His redemption, forgiveness of sin.'

I know that all my sins—the ones I have already committed and the ones I may still commit—have been, ''according to the riches of his grace,'' forgiven. In Christ Jesus I have eternal forgiveness of sin.

Whether saved or lost, I want you to see three things about the forgiveness of sins: (1) the basis of it; (2) the completeness of it; (3) the manner of it.

I. THE BASIS OF FORGIVENESS

There is a reason why God can forgive us of our sins. The Bible says that God shall by no means pardon the guilty. There is not a person who is not guilty before God. The Bible paints a horrible picture of this guilt. ''. . .in my flesh,) dwelleth no good thing.'' ''There is none righteous, no, not one''! ''All have sinned, and come short of the glory of God.''

When God looks at you, He sees you not as your loved ones and friends see you; but He pulls off all the covering and veneer and looks into the innermost pollution of your soul and says, ''The heart is deceitful above all things, and desperately wicked: who can know it?'' God puts one big blanket of condemnation over all the world and says the whole world has sinned. Then the Bible says, "That every mouth may be stopped, and all the world may become guilty before God.''

You are a sinner before Him.

How can God forgive sins of people like us? There must be a basis. If a child does wrong and is brought before his parents, only a weakling of a parent would say, with no basis, no punishment, "That's all right, Son; think no more of it. You are forgiven." What kind of a generation of children would that produce?

Now a holy God is "of purer eyes than to behold evil, and canst not look on iniquity" (Hab. 1:13).

Put over here a holy God, a God of light, a God of justice, a God of infinite purity; put over there us who are sinners, corrupt, vile and weak. How can we bring these two together? What basis is there for God to say, "Thy sins are forgiven"? How can that be?

The problem is expressed in Romans 3:26, ". . .that he might be just, and the justifier of him which believeth in Jesus.'' How can He be just and the Justifier of him that believeth?

Suppose this were a courtroom. Here stands a criminal, guilty of murder, as all of us are. The world is guilty of the crucifixion of the Son of God, and those who are lost will meet God with the guilty, murderous act of the crucifixion of Jesus held against them.

Suppose a judge, in dealing with this criminal, says, "We are going to put the case out of court. We know that you did wrong, but we forgive you and will think no more of it." You would say, "What a weakling that judge is; no basis for it whatsoever."

Does God have a basis for forgiving us of our sins? Isaiah 53:6 says, "All we like sheep have gone astray; . . .and the Lord hath laid on him the iniquity of us all." So the cross, the death of Christ and the blood atonement are the basis of the forgiveness of sin.

Some of you Christians, whether you will admit it or not, often wonder, "Am I truly saved? Am I truly forgiven?" A lack of understanding of the basis of forgiveness causes confusion and doubt, uncertainty and insecurity. So every Christian should want to know what the Bible teaches as the reason God can forgive me of my sins.

On the cross, the Lord had "laid on him the iniquity of us all." When Jesus died, my sins, your sins, were laid on Him. In the death of Jesus, I see sin condemned, the law of God's mighty Book completely magnified, the sinner saved and the adversary confounded.

On the basis of the cross-work of Christ, God can say to anyone today, "Thy sins are forgiven." So when you think on the forgiveness of your sins, remember it is only the basis of the cross of Christ; for God can look upon that cross-work and say, "The sins of that man have been atoned for, paid for, died for. On that basis, I can forgive him if he accepts that by faith."

Somebody has to suffer for sin. Remember that. If you will not accept the suffering of Christ, then you will have to do your own suffering. Someone has to pay. "The wages of sin is death." Therefore, for sin someone has to suffer, to die. It is up to you whether it be you or Christ.

I read a beautiful and true story of an incorrigible young boy attending camp in Canada. Nobody could do anything for or with that boy, yet they thought at this camp he perhaps could be helped.

A good Christian man there vowed to help him. "By the grace of God, I will succeed in straightening out that incorrigible boy!"

One day this boy did something terribly wrong. The council wanted to send him home as a lost cause. But the Christian man said, "Let me take this boy to my cabin. Lock us up for an hour. After that time I'll let you talk to him again. Then we will decide whether to send him home." The council agreed.

Inside his cabin, the good man sat down and said, "Now, Son, you have done wrong. You have sinned and broken every law in this camp. The whole council has agreed that if you got what was coming to you, you would be sent home today. Son, somebody has got to suffer for what you have done." He then pulled off his coat. The boy's eyes got big, then they filled with tears. The man pulled off his shirt and laid it aside. He took the belt off his trousers, folded it, took hold of one end and said, "Son, somebody has got to suffer."

The young man said to himself, *Yeah, another beating!*

But the good man handed his belt to the boy, turned his back to him and said, "Lay it on me. Go ahead; lay it on me."

The boy said, "Oh, no, Sir; I wouldn't hurt you." The Christian said, "Son, somebody is going to get a beating in this room—me or you. For you to get one won't solve your problems. If you pay for your sins, it by no means will solve your problems. If you reject Christ, you will spend eternity in Hell."

Finally that boy, timidly at first, began to hit the naked back of the good man as he was instructed to do. He laid several lashes on him. Then as the good man put on his shirt, belt and coat, a trembling, quivering, broken, repenting boy fell in his arms.

He went back to the council and said, "He's a new boy now."

Oh, thank God for Calvary! That is the basis of it. God laid upon Him the lashes due me! That is why God can forgive you today, and THERE IS NO OTHER REASON. God forgives us on the basis of the cross-work of Jesus Christ.

"Thy sins are forgiven."—Luke 7:48.

II. THE COMPLETENESS OF FORGIVENESS

The Devil likes to make us Christians believe that our forgiveness is only partial. You might look at your sins as in two different groups—that group of sins before you were saved and that group of sins after you were saved. Some of you know God has forgiven you of your sins before and after you were saved, but you have never forgiven yourself for some of them. So you look at them in two groups.

A lady in the prayer room may exemplify just what I am

talking about. Her problem on forgiveness was that she did not really know that she was saved. She said something like this: "Mr. Malone, this is what bothers me. I can see how the Lord can forgive me of all my sins prior to tonight. Tonight I came forward to be saved and to accept Christ! But I know I am still living in the world of sin, living in a home with an unsaved husband and working in a world of unsaved people. What am I going to do about my future sins?"

Thus, she expressed the problem that many of you worry about. "What about the sins I have not committed yet? What about forgiveness of those?"

I said to her, and I say to you, "When Christ died, all of your sins were future. Even the ones in your past were future and uncommitted. When Christ died on Calvary, He died for both groups of sins, past and future. So the forgiveness of God is absolute and complete. This is one of many reason why I'm glad to be a Christian."

Of course our daily sins must be confessed to God. Otherwise you will lose fellowship, communion and power with Him. First John 1:9 states, "If we confess our sins, he is faithful and just to forgive us our sins, and to cleanse us from all unrighteousness." Now why does that verse say He is "faithful and just" instead of saying, "If we confess our sins, he will be *gracious* and *merciful* to forgive us"? He is "faithful and just" because Christ on the cross died for all my sins, including my future sins; and when I come to God, He owes it to me through Christ, to forgive me of whatever sin I confess to Him. In order to be faithful and just, God must forgive me for whatever I ask of Him.

That wonderful verse is for the believer who has sinned against God after becoming a Christian.

III. THE MANNER OF FORGIVENESS

The third most important idea in the Bible concerning the forgiveness of sin is the manner of forgiveness. A woman, a notorious sinner, came to Jesus. She had such guilt and sin that she could not even kneel in front of Jesus but knelt behind Him. The tears were flowing as she bathed His feet with a costly ointment. Then she let down her long strands of hair—a woman's glory—and wiped His feet. Jesus looked down at her and, when He saw the repentance and humility of her heart, said, "Thy sins are forgiven."

An ancient Pharisee—there are many, both modern and ancient—said within himself, 'How could He forgive that woman of her sins?' Jesus, knowing his thoughts, told this story of two men, one of whom owed fifty pence and one of whom owed five hundred pence, and the creditor "frankly forgave them both" (Luke 7:42).

And the Lord asked, "Which of them will love him [the creditor] most?" Simon the Pharisee answered, "I suppose that he, to whom he forgave most." Then Jesus said, 'The woman is so thankful because she was forgiven of so much.'

God freely forgives without reservation, without murmuring.

Think with me, in closing, about Luke 15, a most wonderful chapter in the Bible on forgiveness.

We find here the parable of the lost sheep, the parable of the lost coin, and the parable of the lost boy. In each of the three instances, a lost thing is found. First, the shepherd looks for his sheep until he finds it. The shepherd reaches down and takes hold of the front feet of the sheep, then takes hold of the back feet and swings it up on his shoulders. Here he is on his way home. This is the picture of the Shepherd of my soul and yours.

The shepherd found that which was lost. What was his attitude? He doesn't say, "You had no business running away. I should have left you on the mountainside to perish." No. This shepherd is a picture of Jesus, and Jesus doesn't act that way toward His own. This shepherd comes back rejoicing that he found his beloved lost sheep. He rubs its little head with medicinal oil and says, "You are forgiven. I love you as well as the rest." That is the way God deals with us.

There was a lost coin. A woman lit a lamp and sought diligently until she found it. What did she do? Squeeze her hand and say, "Why, you thoughtless little object! For all the trouble you caused me, I should have left you lost forever"? Oh, no! She calls to her neighbor, "Come, come! Let us rejoice together. I have found that which was lost." Now there is happiness and rejoicing and contentment.

There was a lost boy. This is close to home because a human soul is involved. The prodigal's father, who had been looking for his son, sat on his porch and looked down across the little country road, the meadows and the fields. Then as he was thinking, *Perhaps today he'll come*, he sees an old ragged tramp in the distance shuffling along the road.

The father shaded his eyes. After awhile, he said, "It looks like my son—but it couldn't be. Why, my boy is a better looking young man! No, it couldn't be." He keeps looking. Soon the old father very laboriously rises from his chair, leans on his cane, and as he sees the young man coming closer says, "Why, he is my boy!" Now the father runs as fast as he can to meet him.

We find in this beautiful symbol the only picture in the Bible where God ever runs, where God is ever hurried. God could have made the world and everything in it in six seconds, let alone six days. But He took His time. Now when God sees a sinner coming to Calvary, He actually gets in a hurry to get to him! The old man ran, fell on his son's neck, kissed him and said, 'Son, I'm so glad you are home! Oh, so glad!'

The prodigal was trying to confess, "Father, I have sinned against heaven, and in thy sight, and am no more worthy to be called thy son." But his father interrupted: "Hush, my boy!" and, turning to the servant, said, "Bring forth the best robe, and put it on him; and put a ring on his hand, and shoes on his feet: And bring hither the fatted calf, and kill it; and let us eat, and be merry: For this my son was dead, and is alive again; he was lost, and is found."

This is exactly how God forgives man of his sins. There is no halfway job. The manner of God's forgiveness is absolute, complete, eternal; and He gives it without a murmur, without a grudge.

Forgiveness like that is worth all of the most serious thinking of your ability. It is worth your heart, your soul, your body—all that you have. "Thy sins are forgiven."

Can this be true of you? Do you know today that there is not one sin on your account in the Glory? I do. Not because I am a good man; I am not. I am a sinner saved by God's grace. But my sins have all been charged to Jesus, and I have accepted Him. The payment has been made in full, and I have the receipt both in my heart and in my hand—the Bible.

"Thy sins are forgiven"! That is the most wonderful news you will ever hear.

Chapter XII

Jesus at the Door of Your Heart

(Preached at the Emmanuel Baptist Church, Sunday morning, January 27, 1963)

"Behold, I stand at the door, and knock: if any man hear my voice, and open the door, I will come in to him, and will sup with him, and he with me."—Rev. 3:20.

In Revelation seven messages are written to seven different churches, messages given to John. I am reading the seventh and last of these messages, the message to the church at Laodicea. In your Bibles you may see a heading that reads, "The final state of apostasy." It is believed by some that this is a description of the church in the world in the end times, at the time of the coming of the Lord.

In verse 14 is something about which many have been deceived. A group of people used to call themselves the "chosen one hundred and forty-four thousand"; but since they outgrew that number, they have had to expand their thinking a bit. I refer to the so-called "Jehovah's Witnesses." They are not "Jehovah's Witnesses" but "Russellites." They are kind of like "Grape-Nuts"—neither grapes nor nuts. They are not witnesses to the Truth and do not belong to Jehovah, in my honest opinion.

One of the great doctrines of the "Jehovah's Witnesses' " teaching is that the Lord Jesus Himself was created. They do not believe that He was the Creator but that He was a created being.

Get into a discussion with one (you might as well save your breath), and he will refer to Revelation 3:14, "These things saith the Amen, the faithful and true witness, the beginning of the creation of God." They say Jesus is the first thing God created.

That is not true for several reasons and contrary to many other verses in the Bible. Says John 1:1, "In the beginning was the Word, and the Word was with God, and the Word was God." That verse teaches that Jesus made everything that was made. Jesus is just as eternal as God the Father. This verse doesn't say nor mean that Jesus was the first thing God ever made.

In the original Greek language, "beginning" means the "activator" or the "originator." Judge Russell claimed to be a Greek scholar. When on the witness stand he was asked if he could read Greek. He said, "Yes."

They said, "Then read some." They gave him a book, and he couldn't read it.

"Then say the Greek alphabet." He didn't even know the Greek alphabet.

Judge Russell died like an imposter ought to die—a nervous, toothless old man, a false prophet without God and without hope.

John 1:1 means "the activator," the "originator" of the creation of God. One of the main tenets of "Jehovah's Witnesses'" teaching is absolutely false.

And, like all cults, they deny punishment of the lost. "There is no such thing as an eternal Hell," they argue.

My subject today is "Jesus at the Door of Your Heart." Our text says, "Behold, I stand at the door, and knock: if any man hear my voice, and open the door, I will come in to him, and will sup with him, and he with me."

It is interesting to see in the Bible that, after Jesus arose from the dead and forty days later ascended back into Heaven, He made only two appearances after His ascension. He appeared at least a dozen times between the resurrection and the ascension; but after Jesus arose, He appeared only two times in the heavens to people.

He appeared to the Apostle Paul. Acts, chapter 9, gives the record where Paul, lost and without hope, one day walked the Damascus road without God. A white light from Heaven struck him to the ground; and a voice said, "I am Jesus whom thou persecutest." And Saul was gloriously and miraculously saved by the appearance of Jesus in the heavens after He had ascended. Paul saw the Lord. Ananias said to Paul in verse 17, "The Lord, even Jesus. . . appeared unto thee in the way." And Paul said in I Corinthians 9:1, "Have I not seen Jesus Christ our Lord?"

Some sixty years after Jesus had been on earth, had died on the cross, had risen from the grave and had gone back into Glory, He appeared the second time. This time it was to John on the Isle of Patmos. After sixty years of being in Heaven, Jesus appeared to John and gave him the message and all the teaching of the book of Revelation. In this book that Jesus gave to John sixty years after His death, Jesus seems to be saying to John, "This is the picture of Myself that I want you to give to men and women: 'Behold, I stand at the door, and knock.' "

Here you see where Jesus is today. I know that doctrinally, theologically, technically, Jesus is seated at God's right hand in Heaven at the throne of God; but He is saying, "John, I want the world to have this picture of Me: 'Behold, I stand at the door, and knock.' "

The third appearance of Jesus, since His ascension into Heaven, will be as recorded in Hebrews 9:28, "Unto them that look for him shall he appear the second time without sin unto salvation." That will be when the Lord comes for His own.

This morning I could talk about WHY Jesus knocks, about WHEN Jesus knocks at the heart's door; but I would like to speak on HOW Jesus knocks.

How does He knock? There are five distinct and different ways that Jesus knocks at the heart's door of men and women.

I. HE KNOCKS THROUGH SORROW

Jesus often comes to the door of the human heart, stands outside and gently knocks and waits for an entrance; and He does it through sorrow.

For instance, there was Naaman. Had Naaman not been a leper, he would never have met the Prophet Elisha. Had Naaman not been a leper, he would never have been a Christian. It was because of an incurable disease and the sickness and loss of health that he was brought into contact with the Son of God. His leprosy was cleansed, and he was saved. Had he not been a leper, he would never have met the Lord.

Another example of this was the man at the pool of Bethesda. He went to that pool wanting healing. One day Jesus came to that pool, looked at that man and said, 'Man, wilt thou be made whole?'

And this man said, "Sir, I have no man, when the water is troubled, to put me into the pool."

Jesus said to that man, "Rise, take up thy bed, and walk." And he was gloriously healed.

Had that man not been at the pool, had he not been born a cripple, had he not needed the healing touch, he would never have been saved.

Jesus knocked at Naaman's heart through the disease of leprosy. He knocked at the door of the heart of that man at the pool of Bethesda through crippled limbs and his affliction.

John, chapter 9, tells of a blind man. One day Jesus spat upon the ground and made a divine ointment of clay and spittle. That blind man said, "One thing I know, that, whereas I was blind, now I see."

Here is one who came to know Jesus. Why? Listen and you will know why. One day the disciples asked Jesus, "Master, who did sin, this man, or his parents, that he was born blind?"

Jesus answered, "Neither hath this man sinned, nor his parents: but that the works of God should be manifest in him."

Had he not been blind he would never have been saved.

That is why I say to you this morning that Jesus stands at the door and knocks.

He knocks through sorrow.

I read a great sermon on this subject by Dr. L. R. Scarborough, who was once president of the great Southwestern Baptist Seminary in Fort Worth, Texas. He was also a great preacher and soul winner. I wish there were more Southern Baptists now like Dr. Scarborough.

He was holding a revival meeting many years ago in a city in Texas. One night only about seventy-five people came. In this cowboy town, Dr. Scarborough had been out that day mixing and mingling with the cowboys, trying to get acquainted with them and win them. That night, sure enough, one came. With his cowboy boots and chaps on, wearing a cowboy shirt, and his hat in his hand, he came into the meeting and sat down near the back.

In his sermon that night, Dr. Scarborough preached for the soul of that man. When he gave the invitation, the cowboy made no response. He went back where he was sitting, got him by his right arm and said, "Cowboy, I want you to be a Christian. I want you to be saved."

That cowboy jerked his right arm out of his hand, stalked out of the church and went on his way.

The next morning he got on his horse. He was riding along when the horse fell and pinned his right arm under the body of the horse and broke his arm.

That night he came back to the meeting. He came down the aisle with his broken arm in a sling and said, "Preacher, last night I wrenched this broken arm from your grip. I turned my heart against Jesus Christ and walked out of this building. I would like to give that right arm to you tonight, but I can't. So I'll give you my left arm. I want to be saved. God spoke to me, under the body of that horse, with that right arm that I had wrenched from your hand. I said to Him, 'If You will let me be rescued from under this fallen horse, I'll be saved tonight.' Here I am!''

Not all sickness and sorrow is sent to punish people. But He stands at the door and knocks many times in the time of sorrow. Had some of you not had one of your children get sick, I believe you would never have been saved. Had some of you never gone yonder to the hospital and been put under an anesthetic and gone into the operating room and down into the deep dark valley near the door of death, you would never have been saved.

"Behold, I stand at the door, and knock." He knocks through sorrow and tears.

II. HE KNOCKS THROUGH HIS SAINTS

In Revelation 22:17 we read, "And the Spirit and the bride say, Come." The "bride" is the church, that is, saved people. Writing to the church at Corinth, Paul, in II Corinthians 5:20, says, "Now then we are ambassadors for Christ, as though God did beseech you by us: we pray you in Christ's stead, be ye reconciled to God."

God knocks at the heart's door through His saints. If God has placed in your home a born-again Christian, if God has placed in your family someone who is saved, God put him/her there as a witness and an ambassador to bring you to Christ. Every testimony, every prayer, every tear, every witness, every pleading from him to you, is Jesus knocking at your heart's door.

The great evangelist Sam Jones sat one day in a depot beside a traveling salesman. Sam Jones began to talk to the salesman. He asked him if he was a Christian. The man immediately began to weep. "Yes, I am. I am saved. And let me tell you how I got saved.

"When I left home many years ago, my Christian mother said, 'Son, I will pray for you to be saved as long as God gives me breath.' During all these years my mother has written me, and in every letter she says, 'Son, I want you to be a Christian.'

Every letter is filled with the story of the Gospel. She wants me to be saved.

"But when I got her letter a few days ago—mother is seventy years of age—I began to notice not just what it said, but I saw the shaking, trembling, scribbled writing. As I looked at that letter, all of a sudden the thought came to me: *This may be the last one. She has written me all through these years and pleaded with me about my soul. Now this may be her last letter.*

"When I saw the weariness, realized the age, saw the tears in this writing, I wrote her this: 'Mother, when I read your letter, I got down on my knees and surrendered my heart to Jesus Christ. Mother, I'm sorry I have waited all these years; but I want you to know that your son is now a Christian.' "

Year in and year out the prayers of that godly mother followed that lost boy across the country. Every Christian loved one is Jesus knocking at your heart's door.

In chapter 1 of Proverbs there is a heart-searching passage of Scripture. God says:

"Because I have called, and ye refused; I have stretched out my hand, and no man regarded; But ye have set at nought all my counsel, and would none of my reproof: I also will laugh at your calamity; I will mock when your fear cometh."—Vss. 24–26.

If you are lost, you go on if you will, go on if you must, turn a deaf ear to the prayers of God's people if you will; go on and ignore their broken hearts; but God says, "Because I have called, and ye refused...I also will laugh at your calamity; I will mock when your fear cometh." Someday God will sit in Heaven and laugh because people would not hear Him when He called.

God calls people; and the gentle knocking of every sweet Christian is like the blood-stained hand of Jesus knocking at your heart's door.

He knocks through His saints.

III. HE KNOCKS THROUGH HIS SPIRIT

The Holy Spirit of God who is omnipresent, who can be everywhere, speaks to the heart. Genesis 6:3 reads, "My spirit shall not always strive with man." That teaches, in the very beginning of this Bible, that the Spirit of God strives with people. I believe there are some in this church with whom the Spirit of God has been striving about your soul. The striving of the Spirit is the gentle but sure knocking of the Son of God at your heart's door. "Behold, I stand at the door, and knock."

Call it what you will, but there is one sin about which JESUS said, 'For this sin, there is no forgiveness, neither in this world nor in the world to come.' What is that sin? In Matthew 12:31 Jesus said, "Wherefore I say unto you, All manner of sin and blasphemy shall be forgiven unto men: but the blasphemy against the Holy Ghost shall not be forgiven unto men."

Jesus said there is a sin against the Holy Ghost for which there is no forgiveness. No wonder Paul wrote, "And grieve not the Holy Spirit of God, whereby ye are sealed unto the day of redemption" (Eph. 4:30).

My friends, sometimes the Holy Spirit of God works silently. He does not speak audibly, but He is at work. Even now, I KNOW the Holy Spirit is speaking to hearts in this room. He works silently, and sometimes He works mysteriously. But remember this: the Holy Spirit is sensitive. He can be grieved. He can be blasphemed against. He can be so sinned against that He will leave and will speak no more.

I have known of people to give up their own loved ones. I read in Romans, chapter 1, three times this expression, "God gave them up." God meant what He said when He said, "My Spirit shall not always strive with man."

You may not be a Christian, and your conscience has told you that you are wrong to reject Jesus Christ. That is the Holy Spirit at work.

A refined southern gentleman lived at the edge of town on a farm. He had only one child—a son. That son became a drunkard and a constant embarrassment to the father. Many was the time he would go to town and bring that drunken son home.

One day he went into town and found the son in the gutter, or he may have been dead drunk in a saloon. At any rate, the farmer took his son by the arm and said, "Son, I want to take you home. Come on now. Let's go home."

The son slung his father from him.

This refined southern gentleman got in his buggy and rode off. When he got home, a servant took his horse and buggy. The father, instead of going into the house, walked down to the hundred acres of woodland that he owned. Some hired hands watched him. He stood there a moment. It seemed as though every muscle in his body was trembling as he lifted his hand toward Heaven and screamed as loud as he could. He put his hands to his sides, stood shaking and shuddering a moment, then lifted his hands toward Heaven and screamed again.

Then when he had regained his composure, he turned and walked to the house. He had no more than stepped on the porch when the son came.

The son walked up to the father and reached out his hands to him and said, "Daddy."

The man turned to the son and said, "No longer are you my son. Go, and never be seen here again."

Ten days later that son died a drunkard in the gutter.

You may criticize that father, but his patience ran out. He came to the end of the line. And down in the woods that day, through the struggle of his soul, he gave up on a drunkard boy.

This Holy Bible teaches that there is a sin which is unto death. God said, "I do not say that he shall pray for it." This Bible says, "Ephraim is joined to idols: let him alone." It says, "God gave them up." Jesus said that there is a sin against God's Holy Ghost for which there is no forgiveness in this life nor in the life to come.

I say it to you kindly as God's preacher; I say it to you because I know I am backed by the authority of God's Word: you may be good to your family, you may be honest and pay your debts; but if you are rejecting and denying the Holy Ghost, you are in grave danger. When Jesus knocks at the heart's door, He does it through the Holy Spirit.

"Behold, I stand at the door, and knock: if any man hear my voice, and open the door, I will come in to him, and will sup with him, and he with me."

IV. HE DOES IT THROUGH THE SCRIPTURE

He knocks through the Bible, the blessed Word of God. Romans 10:17 says, "So then faith cometh by hearing, and hearing by the Word of God." The Bible says that faith comes by hearing this Word. There is no other way to be saved. We read in I Peter 1:23, "Being born again, not of corruptible seed, but of incorruptible, by the word of God, which liveth and abideth for ever."

When Jesus knocks, He knocks through His Holy Word.

Jesus said in John 5:24, "Verily, verily, I say unto you, He that heareth my word, and believeth on him that sent me, hath everlasting life, and shall not come into condemnation; but is passed from death unto life." Every verse of Scripture—be it from a pulpit, in a tract, on a signboard, from the lips of a Sunday school teacher—is the gentle knocking of the Son of God for your soul.

Proverbs 29:1 says, "He, that being often reproved [hears it often] hardeneth his neck, shall suddenly be destroyed, and that without remedy." Jesus knocks through this Word. I plead with you as your friend, as a preacher, as someone who has been saved from sin and Hell, do not go against the Word of God. He knocks through His Word.

V. HE KNOCKS, HIMSELF, AS A SAVIOUR

It is the Saviour knocking and saying, "Behold, I stand at the door, and knock: if any man hear my voice, and open the door, I will come in to him, and will sup with him, and he with me.'' Think of the Son of God. Think of the One outside the door of your heart. Forget about me. Forget this choir. Forget this audience. Forget this church. It is Jesus, the Saviour, knocking!

When Jesus came in obscurity, all that loneliness was for you. When there was no room for Him in the inn, and He was born out in the straw of a stable and laid in a manger, it was for you. When Jesus was hated, when they sought to kill Him even before God's appointed time, it was for you. When Jesus took the cross and put it on His back and walked the bloody mile from Pilot's hall to Calvary's hill, it was all for you. When, the third day, Jesus came out of the grave, arose and conquered death, it was all for you. When Jesus went back into the Glory, took His place at God's right hand and is there to intercede between God and man, it is for you.

Listen to the One who stands outside this morning: it is not just a preacher but Jesus Himself!

If you were to say to me, ''Tom Malone, I never want to hear your voice again,'' that would not mean you would go to Hell. You may say that to me and still be saved. But it is not Tom Malone who says, ''Behold, I stand at the door, and knock.'' It is Jesus Christ, the only One who knocks at your heart's door, who could ever save you.

It may not be true, but I have heard it often that one time in one of our midwestern states, a man was condemned to die for murder. They had sought every excuse in the world to get the governor to pardon him, but all efforts so far had failed. Finally the governor of the state said, ''I will personally go to his cell with a pardon in my pocket. I will talk to him personally and at that time will decide whether he should be spared.''

It is said that the governor, dressed like any ordinary man, went and was led by the warden of the prison to death row. Down past the rows of condemned men he walked until he came to the cell where the man in question was imprisoned, waiting his execution.

The warden unlocked the cell door and let the governor in. He said, "Son, I have come to talk to you about right and wrong. Your life has been wrong. I am a Christian. I came to tell you that God can forgive you. I came to tell you that Jesus died on the cross for all of your sins, and you can be saved. Son, I came to help you."

It is said that the prisoner said, "Now listen. I don't know you. I never laid eyes on you before. I have had chaplains, preachers and priests come to my cell. I have heard all about my need to be saved and the love of Jesus for my soul, but I want no part of it. If you came to talk to me about right and wrong, you might as well leave."

It is said that the governor put his hat on his head, put the piece of paper back in his pocket, walked to the front of the little prison cell and said to the warden, "Let me out."

They closed that cell door and locked it. The governor started down the hall to leave that prison. The warden, who stood and watched it all, came to that door, looked at that prisoner and said, "You are the biggest fool I have ever known!"

"Why?"

"Do you know who stood in this cell with you a few moments ago?"

"No, I never saw him before."

"The man who came into this room and pleaded with you about your soul, talked with you about right and wrong, was the governor of this state and the only human being who could ever save your life and set you free."

It is said that that prisoner took two bars in his hands and a wild look came in his eyes and he screamed, "Oh, my God! I let the only one leave who could have ever liberated me!"

Friend, hear today the knocking, knocking, knocking. You ask, "Who is outside?"

The One who died, robed in blood and crowned with thorns,

says, "Behold, I stand at the door, and knock: if any man hear my voice, and open the door, I will come in to him, and will sup with him, and he with me."

You must open the door. God will never kick it down.

In 1935, in the second week of August, at a little country altar in North Alabama, I heard Him knock. He had knocked often before, but I had turned Him away. He had knocked when I was eleven years old. And for nearly nine years He had been knocking. In that morning service, with less than one hundred people present, He knocked at my heart's door. I knew it was Jesus. I knew that no one could ever open the door but me. I opened it that day! And, thank God, He came walking in! He sat down on the throne room of my soul. He now lives in my body.

"Behold, I stand at the door, and knock: if any man hear my voice and open the door, I will come in to him, and will sup with him, and he with me."

Will you listen to that knock today?

Chapter XIII

Why Few Are Saved; Why Multitudes Are Lost

(Preached in 1973)

"Then said Jesus unto the twelve, Will ye also go away? Then Simon Peter answered him, Lord, to whom shall we go? Thou hast the words of eternal life."—John 6:67, 68.

There are two heart-searching questions here: "Will ye also go away?" and, "Lord, to whom shall we go?" We will consider these two questions today.

Jesus performed many miracles. The greatest of them, in many ways, is recorded in John 6. The Bible tells us of certain miracles He wrought such as healing the eyes of the blind, raising the dead on three occasions, and often healing the sick. This Gospel of John says:

"And many other signs truly did Jesus in the presence of his disciples, which are not written in this book: But these are written, that ye might believe that Jesus is the Christ, the Son of God; and that believing ye might have life through his name."—John 20:30, 31.

If all the miracles Jesus did were to be written, the world itself could not contain the books thereof. No one knows how many blind eyes Jesus opened, how many dead Jesus raised, how many times Jesus lifted some sick person by the hand and made him well. He wrought many miracles.

There is one miracle, however, that all four of the Gospels—Matthew, Mark, Luke and John—make a record of in detail—the record of the feeding of the five thousand men, besides women and children. This miracle is related to another miracle Jesus wrought, which is also recorded in the Gospel of John.

In chapter 2 is the miracle of turning the water to wine. This miracle speaks of His blood that would be shed.

Here in chapter 6 He performs another miracle when He takes the loaves and fishes from a little lad and multiplies that lunch so that it feeds thousands of people, with twelve basketfuls remaining. This miracle speaks of His broken body.

Thus we have the two elements that come into prominence when we sit together at the table of the Lord—the blood shed upon the cross for the redemption of man and cleansing from sin and the broken body of our Lord.

I see five thousand men with their wives and children sitting upon the grassy slopes around the Sea of Galilee and beholding with open eyes the greatest miracle the Son of God ever wrought. I see them eat the bread that literally came from Heaven, a miracle direct from the Son of God.

But at the close of this chapter, I do not find what I would expect to find—this great multitude falling at His feet, doing obeisance to Him and acknowledging Him. Rather, I find a strange picture at the close of this chapter.

The great multitude had been divided into two groups—a very large one and a very small one. I see the very large group turn their backs on the Son of God and walk across those grassy slopes back to the communities and cities from which they came. They turn their backs on Jesus and go away from Him.

I also see twelve lonely men stand upon those grassy slopes. As Jesus saw that multitude walk away, He turned to those twelve and asked, "Will ye also go away?"

This picture is set forth in literally dozens of places in the Bible. God divides the human race into two groups. They are not two equal groups, for one is always large, and the other is always small.

That was true in Noah's day, when a large group was destroyed by a flood, and a small group was saved by an ark.

That was true in the days of Sodom and Gomorrah, when a large group was destroyed with fire and brimstone, and a small group was guided by an angel out of the overthrow of God's judgment.

That was true when Jesus looked at those who knew Him during the days of His public ministry and said, "Fear not, little flock; for it is your Father's good pleasure to give you the kingdom."

It was also true when Jesus said:

"Enter ye in at the strait gate: for wide is the gate, and broad is the way, that leadeth to destruction, and many there be which go in thereat: Because strait is the gate, and narrow is the way, which leadeth unto life, and few there be that find it."—Matt. 7:13, 14.

This is true in our day: few are saved; multitudes are lost. This will be true when the Lord Jesus shall return from Heaven. Few, comparatively speaking, will be raptured away, while many will be left behind to suffer the judgment of God.

No wonder the ancient Prophet Joel cried, "Multitudes, multitudes in the valley of decision" (3:14).

You ask, "Brother Malone, can you explain why a great multitude went away from Jesus and only a little group remained with Him?" Chapter 6 of John gives us several reasons why people went away from Jesus. They go away for the same reason they went away two thousand years ago. I see the same scene today that Jesus saw when, with broken heart and tear-stained face, He watched the thousands go away in rejection, then turned to His little school and asked, "Will ye also go away?"

These thousands, yea, millions, must be evangelized.

I. THEY WENT AWAY BECAUSE OF HIS TEACHING

They went away from Jesus then, and they go away from Him now, because of His teaching. I find four things in this chapter which Jesus taught on that day which are hard for people to accept.

1. He Must Be Sought for Spiritual Reasons

On that day Jesus looked at that multitude and said, "Verily, verily, I say unto you, Ye seek me, not because ye saw the miracles, but because ye did eat of the loaves, and were filled." Jesus told them, 'Ye seek Me not because of the miracles I have done; you seek Me merely because you have seen Me feed people. You seek Me for a physical reason, not for a spiritual one.'

When you see people in great crowds today, I would to God you would think of this and discern: "What are those crowds after?"

It is the hunger and prayer and cry of my soul that God would help me preach to as many people as possible; but I ask, "What are those crowds after? Are they looking for the healing of the body?" That might be a good reason, but that is not a scriptural reason for coming. I believe in divine healing and the miracle-working power of God on the human body, but if one comes only to get a well body, he will not get his soul saved nor his sins forgiven.

"Ye seek me, not because ye saw the miracles, but because ye did eat of the loaves, and were filled."

The miracles which Jesus wrought brought many people after Him but very few to Him. And the "so-called" miracles today draw multitudes after Christ but few to Jesus.

"Will ye also go away?"

2. The Father Must Draw Men to Him

In chapter 6 Jesus tells how people can come to Him. There is but one way. Jesus said in verse 44, "No man can come to me, except the Father which hath sent me draw him: and I will raise him up at the last day." No one can come to Jesus except he is drawn of God. He might have his emotions moved and stirred. We need tears and excitement in our preaching and witnessing. We need warm hearts and cool heads. I never want to be one to say I do not believe in tears and emotions in connection with the work of God. Yet one can have his emotions stirred; and, in the midst of excitement, he might have his will moved upon to come to God, but "no man can come to me [Jesus], except the Father. . .draw him."

There is only one way to come to Jesus Christ and only one holy, divine purpose for coming, and that is to come to be saved and to come called of God's Holy Spirit. Any soul-winning ministry must be a Spirit-filled ministry, because only the Holy Spirit can draw men to God.

3. Man Must Partake of Him to Be Saved

Jesus went on with His strong teaching. In verse 53 He said, "Verily, verily, I say unto you, Except ye eat the flesh of the Son of man, and drink his blood, ye have no life in you."

It is not what the Catholic church says it is—the doctrine of transubstantiation, the doctrine that the elements actually turn into the body and blood of Jesus when they are partaken of. We do not believe that. We do not believe that Jesus spoke literally when He said, "Except ye eat the flesh of the Son of man, and drink his blood, ye have no life in you." We believe that Jesus here is saying that except you partake of the Son of God and He becomes a part of you and comes to live in your temple, your body, as your Saviour, you have no life in you.

In order to be saved, one must be "partakers of Christ" (Heb. 3:14) and "partakers of the divine nature" (II Pet. 1:4).

"That is strong teaching, Jesus, and it may cause You to lose Your crowd." True evangelism is that which brings people to a personal Christ and not merely to a program or denomination.

4. The Flesh Profiteth Nothing, but the Spirit Quickeneth

In verse 63 Jesus made the strongest statement that any teacher or preacher could ever make: "It is the spirit that quickeneth [or maketh alive]; the flesh profiteth nothing."

It is the Spirit of God that gives life; and without the Holy Spirit, the flesh and all that it can do profiteth nothing.

Man can join the church, be baptized, sit at the Lord's table, carry a Bible under his arm, engage in religious activity; but without the Holy Spirit in his heart, "the flesh profiteth nothing."

"If any man have not the Spirit of Christ, he is none of his."— Rom. 8:9.

When you hear that kind of preaching and teaching, don't say it comes from a narrow, bigoted and uneducated person; because that is the kind of teaching Jesus did. Strong preaching! He said, 'Seek Me for a holy purpose. You cannot come except God calls you. You must actually partake, for all the flesh is of no avail without the Spirit of God in you.'

The crowds turned and walked away because they objected to His teaching.

There is nothing more nauseating today than to hear a lot of these "so-called" modernists. There is nothing modern about them. They are as old as the day Satan, in his serpentine form, went with subtle unbelief into the Garden of Eden to bring about the fall of the human race. They say, "We believe in the teachings of Jesus, not in a gory, slaughterhouse, bloody religion. We believe in the ethics of Jesus, the teachings of Jesus."

Dear friends, remember it was the Son of God who said, "Ye must be born again." It was the holy, spotless Son of God who said, "Except ye eat the flesh of the Son of man, and drink his blood, ye have no life in you."

Don't you say you believe in the teaching of Jesus unless you believe in salvation through the medium of the bloody cross and the Son of God nailed to it. Don't you say you believe in the teaching of Jesus unless you believe in being born from above by the regenerating miracle of God's Holy Spirit. Don't you say you believe in the teaching of Jesus unless you believe in a literal, bodily resurrection, an empty tomb, an occupied throne, and the coming of Jesus in the clouds of Glory.

The teaching of Jesus is the strongest the world has ever heard. No teacher or preacher ever spoke any stronger than Jesus. No wonder they turned and went away. He spoke in love, but He spoke the Truth.

The Bible tells us that, in our generation, people shall "heap to themselves teachers, having itching ears." They don't desire the truth wholeheartedly. They want their ears tickled, their consciences salved, their hearts appeased but not cleansed.

So they went away.

II. THEY WENT AWAY BECAUSE
OF THE FEAR OF MAN

The wise man of the book of Proverbs said, "The fear of man bringeth a snare: but whoso putteth his trust in the Lord shall be safe" (29:25).

I've seen the fear of man bring a snare in the realm of politics. I've seen men literally sell their souls, their character and their integrity to tie onto their political coattails people and groups of people who might elect them to office.

I've seen it in the realm of business, and so have you. We have seen businessmen literally sell their honor, their character and their good name in order to be a success in business because they were afraid to go into conflict with those who might oppose them.

How true that is in the realm of Christianity! We've seen men and women sell their souls because they were afraid to walk with that little group of twelve while the multitude turned its back and walked away.

People go away from Jesus because of the fear of man.

One of the greatest evangelists this would has ever known was Charles G. Finney, a converted attorney. No other man of his generation ever experienced the kind of revivals he knew. Charles Finney prayed and came along at a time when there was a hunger in America, especially in the northeastern section of our country. When he walked into the plants, machines would stop, and the workers would stand motionless. Many times they would fall on their faces in the factories and stores and begin to cry out to God for forgiveness. He preached with such power that hundreds and hundreds of thousands were swept into the kingdom of God in one area of our country. Oh, how we covet such power!

It is said that at night, when he rode his horse to his destination after a service, he would put the horse in the stable, pull the horse blanket about his shoulders, and there in the barn call on God until the sun came over the hills in the morning. Oh, with what power he preached!

While he preached one night, the Chief Justice of the State of New York came walking down the aisle. He realized that he was not a Christian and, for fear of his political friends, was selling his soul to Hell. He walked down the aisle that night, took the hand of Charles G. Finney and said, "I want to be a Christian." That great Chief Justice asked if he could say a word to the audience. His hair was gray with the snow of many winters, and his shoulders were bent beneath the weight of many years. He faced the audience and said to that multitude, "For fear of my companions-at-law, I have rejected God's Son until this late hour in life. I want to beg you, young or old, right now, no matter what the cost, no matter what people might say, to become a Christian."

It is said that as he stood there with outstretched arms, he became a preacher, he who had just been saved for a moment, and people by the score began coming down all the aisles to be saved.

Dear friend, this text is as true this morning as it ever was: "For

none of us liveth to himself, and no man dieth to himself'' (Rom.
14:7). Your life today casts an influence either for God or against
Him. You today are leading someone—your children, your friends.
You may not lead many, but you lead some. Everyone in this building is a leader, and you shall face your influence at the judgment
bar of God. I beg you, do not go away from Jesus because of the
fear of man and do not fail in soul winning because of the fear
of man.

III. THEY WENT AWAY BECAUSE OF DOUBTS AND QUESTIONS

The Bible tells of people who had doubts and questions. Nathaniel
had a doubt which originated in his head. When Nathaniel saw
Jesus, he said, ''Can there any good thing come out of Nazareth?''
That was not a heart doubt; that was a mind doubt. As Jesus saw
Nathaniel sitting beneath a tree, He called him and proved that
a good thing came out of Nazareth.

Thank God, the Jesus we preach is able to meet and satisfy
honest, intellectual doubts.

John the Baptist had an honest doubt of the heart. He was in
prison awaiting his execution. He had been faithful to God in
preaching the Gospel. He sent a messenger to Jesus to ask an
unanswered question: ''Art thou he that should come, or do we
look for another?''

Jesus removed John's doubt by saying to the messenger, ''Go
and shew John. . . The blind receive their sight, and the lame walk,
the lepers are cleansed, and the deaf hear, the dead are raised up,
and the poor have the gospel preached to them'' (Matt. 11:3-5).

John the Baptist got his doubt settled. Jesus is the only answer
today to the doubts and questions of the human heart.

Thomas had a doubt, an honest doubt. He said, ''Except I shall
see in his hands the print of the nails, and put my finger into the
print of the nails, and thrust my hand into his side, I will not
believe'' (John 20:25). Whether he ever did or not, the Bible does

not say; but Jesus removed his doubts as far as He had removed his sins—the distance of the East from the West.

I have a challenge today for any honest person in the world. If one says, "I am not a Christian today because I have an intellectual doubt in my head or an honest doubt in my heart," I will show you how that doubt can be met head-on and challenged and defeated.

In John 7:17 Jesus said, "If any man will do his will, he shall know of the doctrine, whether it be of God, or whether I speak of myself." To get your doubt overcome, follow what light God has given you. If you are not a Christian, take the step Jesus dares you to take; and if your doubts are not removed, we will never ask you to have anything else to do with it. If you are willing to do the will of God and take one step at a time, I promise you that God will throw light on your pathway and remove every doubt from your head and heart.

People sometimes do not come because of doubts.

"Then said Jesus unto the twelve, will ye also go away?"

IV. THEY WENT AWAY BECAUSE OF PROCRASTINATION

People turn their backs on Jesus because they procrastinate— put it off until another day.

Down in Mexico two words are often said: "manana" (tomorrow) and "siesta" (sleep). They sleep today and put off what ought to be done until tomorrow. Think of all the Mexicans have lost; think of all they might have had; think of all they might have gained if they had not for centuries said, "Wait until tomorrow."

I know of no instrument in the hands of the Devil that has sent more people to Hell and caused more to turn their backs on the Son of God than the words, "Not now, Preacher; some other day."

When I stand up to preach in my pulpit, I often think of a man who sat back there under the balcony on Palm Sunday about four years ago. He lifted his hand for prayer during the invitation and by his uplifted hand indicated he was a lost sinner and wanted us to pray for him.

We prayed. As I remember, someone went and spoke to him. Others came to Christ that day, but he did not.

He was burned to death in an awful automobile and truck accident out on Dixie Highway before the next Sunday. I preached his funeral. His body was shipped to the family graveyard down in the southern hills, but his soul is in Hell.

On Easter Sunday, when the invitation was given, a young man came down the center aisle who is now preaching the Gospel. He grabbed me by the hand and said, "Mr. Malone, you mentioned today a 26-year-old man who sat in this church last Sunday whose funeral you have already preached. God being my helper, that is never going to happen to me. Tell me how to be saved."

Two young men—one is in the pulpit right now and the other is in Hell. Sinner, keep saying "tomorrow" and keep on saying it, and you will go straight to Hell when you die. Christian, keep putting off witnessing to your friends and family, and it is likely you will never win them. One by one they will pass to their Christless guilt and doom.

Write a letter today; make a phone call. Get your loved ones in, for the night cometh when no man can work.

"Will ye also go away?"

I wish I had time to preach another sermon on the next question, "To whom shall we go?"

Shall we go to the modernists? NO. They don't know how to meet the hunger of the human heart.

Shall we turn to the world? NO. When a sinner is dying and turns his face to the wall and looks right in the face of an open grave and an endless eternity, the world has nothing to offer him.

Shall we go to wisdom? NO.

Then to whom shall we go? To the One who is the Fountain of all wisdom.

Shall we go to wealth? NO. We'll go to the One who owns the world and all that is in it—the Son of God.

"Then said Jesus unto the twelve, Will ye also go away? Then Simon Peter answered him, Lord, to whom shall we go? Thou hast the words of eternal life."—John 6:67, 68.

Chapter XIV

Judgment at the Great White Throne

(Preached in Watertown, Wisconsin, on June 10, 1971, at the annual meeting of the Fundamental Baptist Fellowship)

"And I saw a great white throne, and him that sat on it, from whose face the earth and the heaven fled away; and there was found no place for them. And I saw the dead, small and great, stand before God; and the books were opened: and another book was opened, which is the book of life: and the dead were judged out of those things which were written in the books, according to their works."—Rev. 20:11, 12.

No doctrine in the Bible is more neglected than the doctrine of the great white throne judgment which deals with the unsaved.

There is a reason for this. Recent generations have gotten some unscriptural ideas about what God is like. We hear many unsaved people talk about God as a God of love, a God of mercy, a God of grace. God is a God of love, a God of mercy and a God of grace. "He that loveth not knoweth not God; for God is love," says I John 4:8. And the same Bible that says God is a God of love also says that God is holy: "And one cried unto another, and said, Holy, holy, holy, is the Lord of hosts: the whole earth is full of his glory" (Isa. 6:3).

So not only does the Bible say that God is a God of love, but it says that God is a God of holiness. Anyone who reads the Bible honestly will come to the conclusion that God loves sinners but hates sin. The very nature of God demands that He punish sinners. And that is what this great white throne judgment is all about.

We find an all-important question in Genesis 18:25: "Shall not the Judge of all the earth do right?" In order to do right and be consistent with His attributes, God must punish sin. That is what the white throne judgment is about.

This world needs to hear about the judgment of the unsaved. Why? In chapter 3 of Romans is an inspired description of the sinfulness and depravity of man, that man is totally depraved.

"There is none righteous, no, not one"; "There is none that doeth good, no, not one"; "For all have sinned, and come short of the glory of God."

Then in the midst of this chapter, describing the depravity of man, the sinfulness of man, we find this statement: "There is no fear of God before their eyes."

We see it in the masses of humanity today. There is no fear of God before their eyes. People need to fear God. A person who does not have a reverential fear of God has no desire to be saved, no intention of ever settling this sin question.

Should people always be afraid of God? No.

I loved my grandfather who had a great part in raising me. In fact, he raised me several times! I used to sit and look at him. He was an individualist and opinionated—and usually his opinions were right.

He wore high-top shoes, a broad-brimmed hat and a heavy mustache. I never saw another man who even reminded me of him. I loved him, but I had a fear of him. I knew that when he said something, he meant it; and I knew if he ever promised punishment, I would get it.

I believe that must be our attitude toward Almighty God. He is a God of love, but the Bible says, "There is no fear of God before their eyes.'' The Bible says it is a bad thing when people do not fear God.

Why do I preach on the great white throne judgment? Because there needs to be a fear of God. This doctrine of the judgment of the unsaved is misunderstood. Many have the idea that all will stand before the Lord at one time and hear Him say, ''You are lost'' and ''You are saved.'' But that is not the way it will happen. Since there are some Scriptures people don't know how to rightly divide, they come to the conclusion from one verse or another that all, at one time, will stand before God. There is no such thing as a general resurrection, no such thing as a general judgment.

"Marvel not at this: for the hour is coming, in the which all that are in the graves shall hear his voice, And shall come forth; they that have done good, unto the resurrection of life; and they that have done evil, unto the resurrection of damnation.''—John 5:28, 29.

People read that and say, ''There it is. All are going to come out of the grave: some unto the resurrection of life, some unto the resurrection of damnation.''

That verse does say that, but between these two resurrections are more than a thousand years. The first resurrection will take place when Jesus comes, and the dead in Christ are brought out of the graves; the second resurrection will take place at the end of the millennium, when God has His great white throne judgment set, and the unsaved dead will then be raised to stand before God.

It is a misunderstood doctrine.

This doctrine of the judgment of the unsaved dead helps us to see God's attitude toward Christ-rejection. God does not take lightly people's rejecting His Son and setting Him at naught, trampling His precious blood under their feet, refusing His offer of mercy. ''He that believeth on him is not condemned: but he that believeth not is condemned already, because he hath not believed in the name of the only begotten Son of God'' (John 3:18).

An unsaved person is sitting today under the condemnation of Almighty God. How important this doctrine is! This is the last great act of God. You can study prophecy, study what God is going to do, in chronological order, but this is the last thing God will do. After this white throne judgment, I read these words:

"And I saw a new heaven and a new earth: for the first heaven and the first earth were passed away; and there was no more sea. And I John saw the holy city, new Jerusalem, coming down from God out of heaven, prepared as a bride adorned for her husband.''—Rev. 21:1, 2.

After this, time shall be no more. After this, eternity sets in. After this, not one soul can ever be saved. After this, there is Heaven just for the saved throughout all eternity. After this, there is nothing but eternal damnation for all those who are not saved. This is God's last great act, and it brings to an end what man calls time. The new Jerusalem descends after this.

This shows God's full execution upon the Edenic curse. Read the history of man, the history of sin, the story of where Adam and Eve fell in the garden—you see that God placed a curse on several things.

First, He placed a curse upon the woman. In this opening part of the Bible, a woman was talking to the Devil when she had no business doing so. God made man first and in His own image. He took woman from the side of man and made her not in God's image but in man's image. And God made man the head of all His creation. Satan comes, the woman talks to him, and, as a result we have the fall of man.

God pronounces a curse upon the woman. ''Unto the woman he said, I will greatly multiply thy sorrow and thy conception; in sorrow thou shalt bring forth children; and thy desire shall be to thy husband, and he shall rule over thee'' (Gen. 3:16). That has been true through all the history of the human race.

God pronounced a curse on the Devil also: "...and between thy seed and her seed; it shall bruise thy head, and thou shalt bruise his heel" (vs. 15).

God will execute that curse. Although the Devil is on the loose today, he is a defeated foe; and the result of this battle between God and the Devil is an inevitable one. God someday is going to say to just one angel, 'Bind him with chains, and put him in the bottomless pit.' He will be there a thousand years, then be released for a little time. There will be further war; then God will put him back in the bottomless pit. God said that he—the Devil—will be tormented day and night for ever and ever.

God is going to torment the Devil forever. There will be no reign, no authority in Hell, not even by the Devil. God will execute His curse upon Hell.

In that fall in Eden, God placed a curse upon man. In Genesis 3:17-19 we read:

"Thou shalt not eat of it [the tree]: *cursed is the ground for thy sake; in sorrow shalt thou eat of it all the days of thy life; Thorns also and thistles shall it bring forth to thee; and thou shalt eat the herb of the field; In the sweat of thy face shalt thou eat bread, till thou return unto the ground; for out of it wast thou taken: for dust thou art, and unto dust shalt thou return."*

God not only placed a curse on man but on the ground and on this earth. When Jesus died on the cross, He bore these curses in the crown of thorns which was placed upon His brow. At the close of the Bible, we see a holy God who cannot break His word and who always must do as He said—execute these curses.

Our text says, "The earth and the heaven fled away; and there was found no place for them." It doesn't say that Heaven and earth were shaken and moved; it says Heaven and earth were done away with. God's curse on the earth is being executed.

If he will not come to Christ, the curse on man will be executed at that judgment day. Man will stand before God at the great white throne judgment and be judged.

There are many judgments in the Bible. Some say that there are seven; there might be even more.

There is the judgment of believers' sins on Calvary. "All we like sheep have gone astray; we have turned every one to his own way; and the Lord hath laid on him the iniquity of us all" (Isa. 53:6). So the believers' sins have already been judged.

There is a judgment called self-judgment. When one sits in judgment on himself and settles it, God does not judge it anymore. It is like Paul said, in writing to the Corinthians, "Yea, I judge not mine own self. For I know nothing by myself; yet am I not hereby justified: but he that judgeth me is the Lord" (I Cor. 4:3, 4).

Another judgment is called the judgment seat. Only Christians will stand at the judgment seat and have their works judged. "For we must all apear before the judgment seat of Christ; that every one may receive the things done in his body, according to that he hath done, whether it be good or bad" (II Cor. 5:10).

Then there is the judgment of angels. Angels fell when Satan was cast out of Heaven, and Peter said in II Peter 2:4, "God spared not the angels that sinned, but cast them down to hell, and delivered them into chains of darkness, to be reserved unto judgment."

There is a judgment for the nation of Israel. God has deposited in Israel His oracles of truth. Their loins, humanly speaking, produced the blessed Christ of God. God has been good to Israel, but He is going to judge her one day.

There is the judgment of sinners, and that is the one I am reading about.

"And I saw a great white throne, and him that sat on it, from whose face the earth and the heaven fled away; and there was found no place for them. And I saw the dead, small and great, stand before God; and the books were opened: and another book was opened, which is the book of life: and the dead were judged out

of those things which were written in the books, according to their works.''—Rev. 20:11, 12.

I want you to see some truths about the judgment of people who will not give their hearts and lives to Christ and receive Him as their personal Saviour.

I. THE JUDGMENT THRONE

First is the judgment throne or the great white throne—great in contrast to any other throne the world has ever known and great in contrast to other thrones mentioned in the Bible. ''Let us therefore come boldly unto the throne of grace, that we may obtain mercy, and find grace to help in time of need'' (Heb. 4:16). Come to the throne of grace and find mercy.

This, however, is a great white throne, not a throne of grace, because there will be no grace in it. There will be no mercy there, no tolerance there; there will not be another chance there. This is the last throne; and because it stands for justice and purity, it will be a great white throne.

Hundreds of years before Jesus was born, Daniel took his prophetic telescope, looked down across the unborn centuries and said, ''I beheld till the thrones were cast down, and the Ancient of days did sit, whose garment was white as snow, and the hair of his head like the pure wool: his throne was like the fiery flame, and his wheels as burning fire'' (Dan. 7:9).

Daniel had seen a great throne. He had seen that great image that pictured the four great Gentile kingdoms. He saw the kingdom of Babylon, then Greece and Media Persia, then the great Roman empire. Daniel saw thrones in the making. He saw the throne of Babylon, ruled over by Nebuchadnezzar who conquered the whole world. He saw Belshazzar assume that throne and in his pomp and unbelief rule with a rod of iron over the whole world. Daniel said, 'I see a day when thrones like this and every other throne will be destroyed, and only one will remain'—the great white throne judgment.

It is inevitable that men must stand before the throne of God.

A great museum in Istanbul, Turkey, contains, among other things, the most costly group of jewels to be found anywhere in the world—an accumulation of jewelry and finery of all the Persian sultans of history. We see there a great throne built, a throne literally filled with all kinds of precious gems—no human mind can evaluate the wealth of that throne—yet that sultan who had it made is dead and lies in its dust and ruins.

All thrones will perish, but God's Word said that there will be a great white throne judgment.

"I beheld till the thrones were cast down, and the Ancient of days did sit, whose garment was white as snow, and the hair of his head like the pure wool: his throne was like the fiery flame, and his wheels as burning fire. A fiery stream issued and came forth from before him: thousand thousands ministered unto him, and ten thousand times ten thousand stood before him: the judgment was set, and the books were opened."—Dan. 7:9, 10.

God's Word tells of a great white throne, and He who sits upon it will have such fiery indignation in His face against sin that Heaven and earth will flee away. But sinners must meet Him at the judgment day.

Yes, there will be the judgment throne.

II. THE JUDGE ON THE THRONE

I would not only like for you to see the judgment throne but the Judge on the throne. God is a Trinity—Father, Son and Holy Spirit—but God is going to let Jesus do the judging: "For the Father judgeth no man, but hath committed all judgment unto the Son" (John 5:22).

The Judge on the throne will be the Lord Jesus Christ, the same Jesus who one night with a little infant wail announced His arrival in the stable among the lowly cattle in a little manger in Bethlehem; the same Jesus who walked gently among men and was in privacy for thirty years of His life, then one day walked out in the River Jordan and was baptized of John; the same Jesus who for three and a half years reached out His hands and begged people to come to Him; the same Jesus who said, "All that the Father giveth me shall come to me; and him that cometh to me I will in no wise cast out"; the same Jesus who said, "I am the bread of life: he that cometh to me shall never hunger; and he that believeth on me shall never thirst"; the same Jesus who said, "Come unto me, all ye that labour and are heavy laden, and I will give you rest."

That same Jesus is going to sit on that throne. At His first coming, He was pictured as a lamb that openeth not His mouth, a lamb that is led before His shearers and is dumb. A lamb does not offer resistance. He was pictured as a lamb when He came to die, because He was a sacrificial lamb.

The same Bible pictures Him now as a lion. When Jesus sits on that throne, He will not sit there as God's lamb but as God's lion. The One on that throne can be no other than Jesus Christ.

Did you ever stop to think of all the great doctrines of the Bible that you cannot separate from the doctrine of the judgment of the unsaved? It is connected with the doctrine of the resurrection. You can connect it with the doctrine of the second coming. It is connected with the doctrine of Hell.

Some who claim to have read the Bible in the original Greek try to come up with some kind of concoction about there being no such thing as an eternal Hell. They have a battle of semantics and argue about *hades* and *sheol*.

It is true that in the Old Testament *sheol* means a great abyss. It could mean a grave but doesn't always mean that. A grave is not always a great abyss. *Sheol* in the Old Testament speaks of the bowels of the earth where God imprisons sinners.

The same is true of *hades* in the New Testament. It speaks of a place. Jesus talked about this place when He told of the rich man and the poor man in Luke 16—one man begging for food at the gate and the other whose table was full of all the bounties of life.

"And it came to pass, that the beggar died, and was carried by the angels into Abraham's bosom: the rich man also died, and was buried; And in hell he lift up his eyes, being in torments, and seeth Abraham afar off, and Lazarus in his bosom. And he cried and said, Father Abraham, have mercy on me, and send Lazarus, that he may dip the tip of his finger in water, and cool my tongue; for I am tormented in this flame."—Luke 16:22–24.

Remember that it was Jesus who said the rich man died and begged for a drop of water. When you come to this judgment, God doesn't use the word *hades* or *sheol*; He says people are going to be put into a lake of fire.

Let no one argue about that, for it is in the Bible. I don't enjoy talking about it any more than talking about a child's having to be punished or someone's having to suffer in surgery, but it is a necessity because it is a divine truth that is unalterable. Sinners must stand before God. "And whosoever was not found written in the book of life was cast into the lake of fire," says Revelation 20:15.

Sheol in the Old Testament and *hades* in the New are God's jail where God keeps men until this judgment. The lake of fire is God's penitentiary. Man stays in God's jail until the day of his trial; then he will be in God's penitentiary forever—no exit, no end, no water, no relief.

Call me an old-fashioned preacher, accuse me of using terms that are antiquated; but I am preaching what the Bible says.

When the Gospel first went to the Gentiles in the days of Simon Peter and the house of Cornelius, Simon said, "And he commanded us to preach unto the people, and to testify that it is he which was ordained of God to be the Judge of quick and dead" (Acts 10:42).

In Acts 24 Paul is standing before Felix, and we read, "And as he [Paul] reasoned of righteousness, temperance, and judgment to come, Felix trembled, and answered, Go thy way for this time;

when I have a convenient season, I will call for thee" (vs. 25).

It talks about the "judgment to come." That is what I am talking about. Felix trembled, but he said, "Go thy way for this time; when I have a more convenient season, I will call for thee." Felix trembled, but Felix did not repent.

You may be afraid of judgment; but unless you do something about it, you will be as lost as Felix was. "And as it is appointed unto men once to die, but after this the judgment."

I heard Dr. Bob Jones, Sr., tell this story of a young soldier in the Civil War. One night before battle, as this young man sat at the fireside with his soldier friends, even in the dim light of the fire they could see by the ashen look upon his face that he was frightened.

One of the older veteran soldiers asked, "What's the matter, Son? Are you afraid to die?"

He replied, "No, I am not really afraid to die, though die I may before the sun goes down tomorrow night."

The veteran said, "Then why do you look so pale? Why are you so ashen? Why are you so frightened?"

In the dim light of that fire, the young man answered, "I will tell you why. I'm afraid of what is going to happen after I die, because I am not right with God."

Death is not the frightening thing, but to die without Christ and to stand at the judgment will be the great tragedy.

"Then said Jesus again unto them, I go my way, and ye shall seek me, and shall die in your sins: whither I go, ye cannot come."—John 8:21.

III. THE JUDGMENT ISSUES

Notice the issues of the judgment. When this second resurrection takes place at the end of the millennium, when all the unsaved dead are raised and stand before God, what will be the issues on the judgment day? What will God condemn these unsaved people for?

Several issues will be brought into focus at the great white throne judgment.

First, the books will be opened, and man shall be judged, "every man according to his deeds" (Rom. 2:6). No unsaved person shall escape meeting his life and wicked deeds at the judgment bar of God. At the great white throne judgment, one of the issues will be the deeds of men.

In speaking of unsaved people, God talks of their wicked work. Even if he is religious, everything an unsaved person can do is wicked before God. If he is not saved, even his religious deeds are an abomination unto God.

Then a man's words will be brought into focus at the judgment of the unsaved. I don't know of a more heart-searching thing than that.

Sometimes people wonder how God can bring every idle word said into judgment. But Matthew 12:36 affirms that statement: "Every idle word that men shall speak, they shall give account thereof in the day of judgment."

How can God do that? God can do anything. There are electronic devices that capture the words of men and preserve them for generations. They can be spoken in secret and amplified to millions. According to Jesus, at the judgment day, man must give an account for every idle word he has spoken.

In Matthew 12, where Jesus gave that statement, He talks about a sin for which there is no forgiveness. If one commits this sin, he shall not be forgiven in this world, nor in the world to come. What is that sin? The sin of blasphemy against the Holy Ghost. "Wherefore I say unto you, All manner of sin and blasphemy shall be forgiven unto men: but the blasphemy against the Holy Ghost shall not be forgiven unto men" (vs. 31). When a man from a wicked heart attributes the work of God to the Devil, he commits blasphemy against the Holy Ghost.

Then Jesus went on to say in verse 36, "That every idle word that men shall speak, they shall give account thereof in the day of judgment."

I read a story some years ago about a man witnessing to a group of young people. One of them said, "Why, for $5.00 I would sign away my hope of ever being saved, ever being forgiven."

It is said that this wise Christian took out of his pocket a five-dollar bill and a piece of paper and said, "Let's see if you really will." (This young man challenged God, and this Christian challenged him.)

The young man said, "What shall I write?"

The old veteran, a wise Christian, said, "Write what you said, 'For five dollars I would sign away my right to ever become a Christian.'"

He began to write, then suddenly put paper and pencil and money down and said, "Sir, you know I didn't mean what I said; I couldn't possibly do that."

I have heard, and you have heard people blaspheme the name of God and take His name in vain. But remember what God said: "Every idle word that men shall speak, they shall give account thereof in the day of judgment."

What will be the issues on judgment day? A man's deeds and a man's words and even his thoughts—these shall be brought into focus. Proverbs 23:7 reminds us, "For as he [man] thinketh in his heart, so is he." You don't have to say it with your lips; just think it with your heart; and if it is against God, it is a wicked thought. Says I Corinthians 4:5, "Therefore judge nothing before the time, until the Lord come, who both will bring to light the hidden things of darkness, and will make manifest the counsels of the hearts." God said that on that judgment day, even the things that have been made secret in the life of an unsaved person, the unspoken counsels of his heart (never even spoken by his lips), he will give an account thereof.

What will be the issues of that day? The secrets of men. "In the day when God shall judge the secrets of men by Jesus

Christ according to my gospel'' (Rom. 2:16).

The main issue of the judgment day will be your relationship to Jesus Christ, what you have done with Jesus.

When people have asked me, ''Preacher, how can you know beyond any doubt you are saved?'' I have often used John 5:24 to answer. There Jesus said, ''Verily, verily, I say unto you, He that heareth my word, and believeth on him that sent me, hath everlasting life, and shall not come into condemnation; but is passed from death unto life.''

Christian, if you have heard God's Word and have believed on His Son, Jesus said you shall not come into judgment. That gives sweet assurance.

If that verse means that a person who has believed shall never come to this judgment, it also means that one who has not believed is bound to come to that judgment, for it is for everyone who rejects God's Son.

Pilate asked the question, ''What shall I do then with Jesus which is called Christ?'' (Matt. 27:22). So the issue of the judgment day will be ''What have you done with God's Son, the Lord Jesus Christ?''

IV. THE JUDGED

Who is going to be judged? Revelation 20:12 answers: ''And I saw the dead, small and great, stand before God.''

Poor people will be at the judgment. Some people think the beggar at the gate in Luke 16 went to Heaven when he died because he was poor. NO! He went to Heaven because he was saved.

Some think that, if they have it rough and live in poverty here, they will escape Hell. No. Unsaved people who never had enough to eat in this world will perish in Hell and never have a drop of water throughout eternity. ''And I saw the dead, small and great, stand before God.''

Afflicted people will be there. Persecuted people will be there. Unsaved people, no matter if they are poor and afflicted here on earth, will be at the judgment throne and be assigned their place in an eternal Hell.

I went to a home some years ago. A lady came to the door. Four or five little children were around her. This bedraggled-looking lady lived in a poor, humble home. The children didn't have sufficient clothing, and they looked emaciated and sickly. "I am Brother Malone, pastor of Emmanuel Baptist Church. I come to invite you to visit our church," I said. Then I went on talking to her about the Lord.

She said, "Now, Preacher, let me tell you something. I'm not a Christian and never have been. My husband is a drunkard; and every Friday night, when he gets his paycheck, he heads for the bar. He drinks up most of it with his drunkard cronies while me and these little children suffer. And he does a lot of other things he ought not do." Then she added, "Preacher, I'm getting my hell right here."

As I heard her tragic story, my heart went out to her. Here was a woman who had borne these children and had been a good wife to this man, but she had felt his beatings, and she had been deprived of the normal things of life. Now she felt she was getting her hell right here on earth. I had to tell that lady, "No, you are not. Unless you get saved, you will have to spend eternity in the same Hell with that drunkard husband of yours."

Of that awful day when men meet God, John said in Revelation 20:12, "And I saw the dead, small and great, stand before God; and the books were opened."

John said little people and great people will be at the judgment. There will be kings, men who have ruled nations, at that judgment. There will be senators, judges, lawyers, potentates. Think of it! Maybe one who has been President of the United States of America will stand at the judgment bar of God and hear Jesus say, "I never knew you: depart from me, ye that work iniquity."

In a previous chapter, when John saw a picture of the coming wrath of God, he said, 'Who can stand before the face of Him that sitteth on the throne?' And he said that, in that awful day when God judges the world, captains and mighty men and rich men shall cry out to the mountains and to the rocks, "Fall on us, and hide us from...the wrath of the Lamb: For the great day of his wrath is come; and who shall be able to stand?" (Rev. 6:16, 17.)

If I am speaking to one who has never come to Calvary and been saved, let me say that you will stand in the white light of His holiness; and every word and thought and secret thing of your life will be in panoramic view across the heavens.

What an awful day! I wouldn't want to stand in the sinner's shoes.

If God could give me power to paint the picture from the Bible in regard to what it means to be lost and without God and without hope and headed toward a judgment bar and an eternal Hell, there would not be one of you unsaved. In fact, if God could help you see the truth that I am talking about, perhaps you wouldn't wait for an invitation but would come now to meet Jesus Christ. If you could see it as it really is—that God is a holy God and a God of wrath who will punish sin—you would come right now to Jesus Christ and make Him your personal Saviour.

V. THE JUDGMENT ITSELF

The judgment itself proves some things. First, that death doesn't end all. Not for mankind. Of all the things God ever made, you are the only thing made in God's image. Man is as eternal as God. You and I are going to live somewhere just as long as God lives.

I heard Dr. Bob Jones, Sr., say that, as he walked along a Florida road by himself, all of a sudden something hit him, something he had known and believed was true but something he had never really pondered on, something that changed his life: "I am going to live just as long as God lives!"

My friends, the judgment proves that death doesn't end all. Remember that you might die today, tomorrow or ten years from now; but on judgment day, you will be raised to stand before God.

The judgment also teaches that God is inescapable. You cannot escape God, though you may think you can.

You may say, "I won't listen to that, Preacher. I don't care if my loved ones pray for me; I don't care how many people knock on my door; I don't care how many tracts I may read or how many sermons I may hear or how many songs I may hear sung; I don't have to respond." You are right; you don't.

Some may say, "I don't want anyone forcing me to be saved." No one could; but I will tell you this: you cannot escape God. Someday you are going to meet God Almighty.

The judgment proves there is no escape. Amos 4:12 warns, "Prepare to meet thy God."

The judgment proves that God is holy and just. He rectifies everything, makes everything all right before the end of time.

The judgment proves that sin must be reckoned with. Romans 6:23 declares, "For the wages of sin is death...." And Galatians 6:7 warns, "Be not deceived; God is not mocked: for whatsoever a man soweth, that shall he also reap."

The judgment proves that sin must be reckoned with. You can't laugh it away. You can't smile it away. You can't keep ignoring it. At the judgment bar of God, you will meet sin head-on.

It is like a man who said to his little boy one time, "Son, when you do something bad, I'm going to drive a nail into that post. When you do something good, I will pull one out."

One day it appeared that the little boy had done so many things right that every nail in the post had been pulled. Then the little boy said to his father, "Daddy, the nails are all gone, but the holes are still there."

You may have forgotten it, but God hasn't. If you are not saved and your sins are not under the blood, you will meet God at the judgment throne. "Be not deceived; God is not mocked: for whatsoever a man soweth, that shall he also reap," warns Galatians 6:7. "For the wages of sin is death," Romans 6:23 reminds us. God says sin must be reckoned with at the judgment bar of God.

Then the judgment teaches that Hell is a reality. No one can estimate how many people are in Hell because of the cults and "isms" in the world today. I am like that country preacher who one time said, "I'll be so glad when all the 'isms' are 'wasms'!" The multitudes engulfed by wicked cults are going to end up in Hell.

The Devil can really sugarcoat his pills so people will take them. He puts a little truth in with a lot of lies, and he puts truth in that is misappropriated. I know people who can quote Scripture by the yard who are going to end up in Hell because they are twisted and confused about who Jesus is.

Some say, "There is no Hell. God is too good." Some say, "We will just be annihilated." The Bible nowhere teaches annihilation. There is not one iota of teaching in the Bible that a person will be annihilated and his suffering will be instantaneous only. God says it is eternal.

A man, who engulfed thousands in one of the most wicked cults, one time was put on a witness stand and asked if he could quote the Greek alphabet. He couldn't even quote the Greek alphabet, but he had been deceiving people for almost a generation by saying, "And the Greek says...."

Listen! You can't get into a battle of words on Revelation 20:15, "And whosoever was not found written in the book of life was cast into the lake of fire." You must take it like it is. God says "lake of fire." You say, "That's figurative language." If that be a figure, then the truth is far worse than the figure. You just make a monkey out of yourself when you speak about figurative language.

It is not figurative. Every time the Bible uses figurative language, the whole context will show that God is using a symbol. Here God's Word plainly says, "And whosoever was not found written in the book of life was cast into the lake of fire."

The judgment itself proves that there is a Hell.

There is not much said about Hell today. When I was a boy and went to a week of revival meetings, one night out of seven the preacher preached a sermon on Hell. He made it hot, long and horrible. And he lifted up Christ and talked about the love of God. People got scared of Hell and ran to Calvary.

"Oh, you preachers use fear as a motive; psychologists say fear is not a good motive," you argue.

It matters not what psychologists say. My grandfather was the greatest psychologist I ever knew. His psychology was, "Tom, if you do that, I'll beat the devil out of you." That scared me!

Someone says, "In this modern age, we don't believe in scaring people. You preachers talk about deathbed stories and God's burning people up and all of that. Fear is not a good motive." But I read in Hebrews 11:7, "By faith Noah, being warned of God of things not seen as yet, *moved with fear*, prepared an ark to the saving of his house; by the which he condemned the world, and became heir of the righteousness which is by faith."

Isn't it a tragedy someone didn't tell Noah about what psychologists believe! He wouldn't have had to build that ark—but then he and his family would have drowned!

You may say, "Fear is not a good motive." But don't you take your little child to the fire and say, "Hot, burn! Hot, burn! Hot, burn! Don't touch, burn"? Don't you take him out where the cars are speeding up and down the road and say, "Now stay out of that street. You get in that street, and a car will hit you"? You want to scare him because you don't want to lose him. Just so, God wants His children to fear Him enough to be saved.

"There is no fear of God before their eyes," declares Romans 3:18. More preaching on Hell would make better Christians. I would to God that we believed it! If we had Christians today who believed in Hell like it is taught in the Bible, we would win a lot more people to the Lord.

One of the most active and faithful members of the Emmanuel Baptist Church came to the altar weeping. She held up her hands in desperation and said, "O Pastor, pray for me. My loved ones are lost. My friends are lost. My relatives are lost. I need a vision of Hell.''

(A preacher can't pray that prayer for others without praying it for himself.) It changed her life. She brought her loved ones and friends down the aisles by the dozens in the next few years. Hell is just a myth in the minds of many people. Jesus said:

"And if thy hand offend thee, cut it off: it is better for thee to enter into life maimed, than having two hands to go into hell, into the fire that never shall be quenched: Where their worm dieth not, and the fire is not quenched.''—Mark 9:43, 44.

Jesus said that one day a Christ-rejecter died, lifted up his eyes in Hell and cried, being in torments.

The great white throne judgment is to settle finally who will be put into Hell. God help us to see it!

The judgment teaches that it is universal. No one will escape.

Acts 17:31 says, ''Because he hath appointed a day, in the which he will judge the world in righteousness by that man whom he hath ordained; whereof he hath given assurance unto all men, in that he hath raised him from the dead.''

God raised Jesus from the dead to guarantee that a day of judgment is coming. That ought to affect your behavior here and now. If you are not saved, surely it would cause you to be saved.

VI. THE JUDGMENT IN PROPHECY

The judgment is in prophecy all through the Bible.

Someone may say, ''I don't believe God is going to judge the world.'' Let's look at the past for a moment. Ecclesiastes 12:14 says, ''For God shall bring every work into judgment, with every secret thing, whether it be good, or whether it be evil.''

Look back across the pages of Holy Writ. One day God judged this world because of its sinful flesh: ''The end of all flesh is come before me; for the earth is filled with violence through them; and, behold, I will destroy them with the earth'' (Gen. 6:13).

Look back at verse 3: "And the Lord said, My spirit shall not always strive with man, for that he also is flesh: yet his days shall be an hundred and twenty years." God sent a flood that destroyed the world: "And, behold, I, even I, do bring a flood of waters upon the earth, to destroy all flesh, wherein is the breath of life" (vs. 17).

One day God looked down upon two cities and, because of their worldliness, destroyed them. God used the Flood to destroy the race because of man's sinful flesh; God destroyed Sodom and Gomorrah because of their worldliness.

There was a time when Uncle Abraham talked to his nephew, Lot. Their herdsmen were arguing because they had so much worldly goods. Abraham said to Lot, "We don't need to quarrel; we are brethren. You go one way, and I will go the other, and we will still be brethren. If you want to go to the mountains, then I will go to the plains. If you want to go to the plains, I will go to the mountains."

Lot began to look around. He saw the wicked cities of Sodom and Gomorrah. The Bible says the men of those cities were wicked exceedingly. But because the plains around them were well-watered, Lot said, 'This is a terrible place for my family but a wonderful place for my cattle. I can get rich in Sodom.' Lot moved in. Lot became mayor of the city. He sat in the gate like a judge.

One day God looked down on those two cities; and when He saw their worldliness and materialism, He rained fire and brimstone down on them from Heaven.

Some folks ask, "Do you believe there is real fire in Hell?" Sure. There is real fire in Heaven, too, for God rained it out of Heaven and destroyed those cities of the plains. At the south end of the Dead Sea, under water, are the remains of Sodom and Gomorrah. The sulphuric atmosphere still prevails around that body of water. Not one blade of grass can grow there. God destroyed those cities like He said He would.

God did judge the world. God did judge it with a Flood.

God did judge it with fire and brimstone.

One day men were judged because of a bloodless religion. "And they said, Go to, let us build us a city and a tower, whose top may reach unto heaven; and let us make us a name, lest we be scattered abroad upon the face of the whole earth" (Gen. 11:4).

Speaking to the Trinity, God said, 'Let us go down and see what the people are doing.'

Man said, "Let us build." God said, 'Let us go down and look.'

When He went down and saw the tower and the efforts of a man to get to Heaven without God, He said, 'Man will never be restrained in anything if he is allowed to do this,' and God struck it to the ground.

"Go to, let us go down, and there confound their language, that they may not understand one another's speech. So the Lord scattered them abroad from thence upon the face of all the earth."—Gen. 11:7, 8.

God judged the world. He judged the land of Egypt. For four hundred long years they kept God's people in bondage, and God said that He would send judgment on the land. As I have walked in that land, I have seen the flies, the insects, the poverty, the blindness, the disease, the ignorance and the sin. Millions are still in a land that God judged.

Will God judge? Yes, He will.

God judged Babylon. Nebuchadnezzar built the city walls so thick that three chariots could race around at one time on top of them. One night the unseen messenger of God wrote on the walls of the palace, "MENE, MENE, TEKEL, UPHARSIN." And the interpretation: "MENE; God hath numbered thy kingdom, and finished it. TEKEL; Thou are weighed in the balances, and art found wanting. PERES; Thy kingdom is divided, and given to the Medes and Persians."

The tinkling of glasses stopped, the flying feet of the dance floor and the orchestra hushed, and God spoke in that night, and Belshazzar was slain.

God declared that Babylon would never be rebuilt, that it would be the home of owls and jackals and night animals. Go view those ruins today. That is just what you find. God is a God of judgment.

Will God judge the world? He has judged nations in the past. Says Proverbs 14:34, "Righteousness exalteth a nation: but sin is a reproach to any people."

I have seen God send judgment on people, and I know it was He who sent it.

I remember a man down in Tennessee whose little daughter died.

(The old-fashioned people used to prepare their own dead for burial. They would send to town for a casket and bring it back home on a wagon. The neighbors would come in and prepare the body for the casket. It was left in the home and the next day taken out and buried.)

They asked the man to go out and chop some wood while they heated the water to prepare the child for burial. Before picking up the ax, this Tennessee man lifted his fist toward God and said, "Yeah! Kill a little baby, but have You ever tried a man? Why don't You come down and fight with a man?"

He reached down, put his hand on the ax handle, and a little insect bit him on the end of the finger. In three days he died of blood poisoning, and died blaspheming God.

A young man said one day, "None of these things are sacred to me. I don't believe in God nor in Jesus nor in the blood nor in Calvary nor in the Holy Ghost."

This fellow took a sheep and waded out into the creek, leaving three friends on shore. He announced, "We are going to have a baptismal service. In the name of the Father, Son and Holy Ghost," and he put the sheep under. When it came up, it struggled and pushed the man down. He fell into the stream with the sheep; and since he couldn't swim, his three companions stood like frozen stones and watched him drown.

When asked, "Why didn't you help him?" they answered, "It was as though bands of steel were around our arms; we couldn't move. We were bound to our tracks that day."

Listen! God judges people. I have seen the intervening hand of God come in judgment. Remember Proverbs 29:1: "He, that being often reproved hardeneth his neck, shall suddenly be destroyed, and that without remedy."

God is going to judge the world.

VII. THE JUDGMENT BOOKS

I close by saying that there were the judgment books. John said, "And the books were opened." Daniel spoke of the books: "The judgment was set, and the books were opened" (7:10).

In those books will be a record of every time you heard the Gospel or felt conviction of the Holy Spirit. There will be a record of every time you had contact with a true believer. There will be a record of every time you procrastinated and said, "Go thy way for this time." In that book will be a record of every promise you ever made to get right with God and didn't. In that book will be a record of every invitation or song you ever heard, of every tear ever shed for your salvation. In that book will be a record of every time you were ever angry at a witness who tried to win you. All will be in the books. And God is an accurate Bookkeeper.

John said, "Another book was opened, which is the book of life." Why is it there? Here will come a man to say, "Lord, I am not unsaved. I did many wonderful works in Your name."

God will say to a recording angel, "Get the little book out and look up his name."

The angel will say, "No such name here."

Jesus will say, "Depart from me...I never knew you."

God has always had the book of life. He had it in Moses' day. When the children of Israel sinned, Moses prayed and sobbed and broke in his statement and said, "Yet now, if thou wilt forgive their sin—; and if not, blot me, I pray thee, out of thy book which thou hast written" (Exod. 32:32). Yes, the books will be there at the judgment. Every word, every deed, every thought, every wasted opportunity, every moment of procrastination, every gospel song you have ever heard, every verse of Scripture will be written in that book.

But, thank God, there will be another book. Years ago I saw that my name was written in that book. When I believed in the blood of Christ, God wrote it down forever. The judgment holds no fear for me, for I was judged at Calvary when Jesus died.

"And I saw a great white throne, and him that sat on it, from whose face the earth and the heaven fled away; and there was found no place for them. And I saw the dead, small and great, stand before God; and the books were opened: and another book was opened, which is the book of life: and the dead were judged out of those things which were written in the books, according to their works."—Rev. 20:11, 12.

Chapter XV

Multitudes in the Valley of Decision

(Preached in the Emmanuel Baptist Church, Sunday morning, March 3, 1968)

"Multitudes, multitudes in the valley of decision: for the day of the Lord is near in the valley of decision."—Joel 3:14.

Literally scores of times "multitudes" are mentioned in the Bible. In the earthly ministry of Christ, more than once, great multitudes gathered around Him. They did not always believe in Him, they were not always friendly to Him, but multitudes gathered around Him.

Because of the great crowds of people gathered by the Sea of Galilee, Jesus stepped into a boat and began to preach the great sermon on the kingdom of God recorded in Matthew 13:2.

Analyze these multitudes. They go in two different directions. Some went away from Him; some went to Him. We read about the division of the great multitudes. "Thou shalt not follow a multitude to do evil" (Exod. 23:2). Multitudes often had evil on their minds.

In John 6 Jesus preached to probably the greatest crowd on any public occasion of His ministry. He preached on the Bread of Life and said, "Except ye eat the flesh of the Son of man, and drink his blood [unless you partake of Jesus Christ inwardly], ye have no life in you." In John 6 we read that great multitudes turned and went away from Christ. Sadly He turned to that little band of disciples and asked, "Will ye also go away?"

But that has not always been the case. Sometimes multitudes are drawn to Christ—drawn to His Word; drawn to His house; drawn to the preaching of the blessed Gospel.

The psalmist said, "For I had gone with the multitude, I went with them to the house of God, with the voice of joy and praise, with a multitude that kept holyday" (42:4).

So of the multitudes, some go to the Lord while some go away from Him.

I give you Bible truths about these multitudes in the valley of decision.

I. MULTITUDES ARE LOVED BY CHRIST

There is a most wonderful statement of Jesus in Matthew 9:36, "But when he saw the multitudes, he was moved with compassion on them, because they fainted, and were scattered abroad, as sheep having no shepherd."

The multitudes moved the heart of Christ. He was moved by their destiny, their departure from Him. He was moved by their destruction and need. Multitudes played on His heartstrings and lay heavily upon His mind.

In our churches today, so many are not concerned about the lost multitudes, those whom God loves. "For God so loved the world . . ."—not just those of you sitting here, not just a little select few, not just a people of one nation nor of one race nor of one color—"God so loved the world, that he gave his only begotten Son, that whosoever believeth in him should not perish, but have everlasting life."

When we read in this Bible of "multitudes, multitudes in the valley of decision," God loved these multitudes enough to give His Son to die on a bloody cross that they might be saved.

What shall the church do about the multitudes that are lost? Narrow it down to our city of Pontiac. When I go to other places, many will ask me, "How many people are there in Pontiac?" At this writing (1968), there are less than 100,000, but all around this city are townships with as many as 35,000 population.

Our church is in the midst of a quarter of a million people! We are literally surrounded by multitudes—"Multitudes, multitudes in the valley of decision" for whom Jesus Christ died and whom God loves. Socialism, humanism, formalism, false cults and many other substitutes will engulf these multitudes unless we reach them.

II. MULTITUDES ARE BEING DECEIVED BY SATAN

That subtle enemy of the human soul has this vast system and program by which he deceives these multitudes. Jesus said in Matthew 7:13, "Enter ye in at the strait gate: for wide is the gate, and broad is the way, that leadeth to destruction, and many there be which go in thereat." Jesus said that road is literally filled with multitudes of Satan-deceived people, multitudes in false religions of every kind. Jesus said, "If the blind lead the blind, both shall fall into the ditch" (Matt. 15:14). Satan's preachers and Satan's churches and Satan's religion are all leading millions to a burning Hell.

If you doubt that multitudes can be lost at one time, just read your Bible. "There is a way which seemeth right unto a man, but the end thereof are the ways of death" (Prov. 14:12). In the days of the Flood there was one man, Noah, who "found grace in the eyes of the Lord." For 120 years God had been striving with people, preaching to them, warning them. And God said, 'My Spirit will not always strive with you.' But for 120 years the Spirit of God did deal with the multitudes across the face of the earth. Only one man and his three sons and their four wives—eight people—went into that ark and were saved. Then with one awful stroke of divine judgment, God destroyed this earth and multitudes went to Hell.

There were Sodom and Gomorrah and the surrounding cities. One day Abraham asked God, 'If I can find 50 in those cities who are genuinely saved, will You spare them?' God said He would. Abraham was skeptical of the testimony of his backslidden nephew Lot and said, 'If I can find 40, will You spare them?' God said He would. Abraham then said, 'If I can find 30 or 20 or 10. . .?' God said, 'Find ten Christians, and I'll spare the multitudes in these cities.'

You know the rest of the story. When not ten Christians could be found, the destroying angel rained fire and brimstone from Heaven, and all the multitudes in those cities went to Hell except one man and his two daughters.

Multitudes are being deceived in America by false religions. The preacher tells you, "Do good and you will be saved." You cannot do good. No one can until he is saved. We have a depraved nature and we need a new birth, a spiritual work that the Bible calls conversion. We need to be washed in the blood. We need to be changed. We need to have sins forgiven.

Satan deceives people by the multitudes.

An old preacher in the British Isles, Rowland Hill, used to tell of one day seeing a man leading a herd of hogs right down the street to an open gate. Rowland Hill went to that man and said, "I saw that bunch of hogs following you. It's unbelievable! How did you get them to do it?"

The man said, "What you didn't see was that little bag of beans under my arm. As I walked along, I kept dropping them. The hogs kept following me and kept looking for the beans and eating them."

Rowland Hill said, "That is just what the Devil does. He drops his little sugarcoated beans and gets the multitudes to follow him to the open gates of Hell."

Millions today are religious but lost. But, thank God, some are being saved out of the multitudes in the valley of decision.

I was saved in a little church where the people said you have to be "borned again." So I got "borned again." John 3:3 says, "Except a man be born again, he cannot see the kingdom of God."

Multitudes are deceived by the Devil.

"Multitudes, multitudes in the valley of decision: for the day of the Lord is near in the valley of decision."

III. FICKLE MULTITUDES

If you don't believe that humanity is fickle, look in the Bible and see for yourself.

In the days of Jesus Christ, "a very great multitude spread their garments in the way . . ." (Matt. 21:8). This was one week before so-called Easter Sunday. It was one week before Jesus arose from the dead. He comes into the city and they say, 'Hail Him! Hosanna in the highest!' He was riding on a little donkey. They took off their coats; they filled the streets with their garments and clothes so that little beast of burden could walk upon them. They cried out, "The King! The King! Hail Him!" Now watch it. In Matthew 26 we read, "And while he yet spake, lo, Judas. . .came, and with him a great multitude with swords and staves."

Six days later they arrested Him. One day they cried, "Hail Him!" In less than a week they cried, "Nail Him!" That is how fickle, how wishy-washy, how vacillating human nature is. The Bible shows us these multitudes can be deceived, misled and misguided.

One thing not found today, as when I was a boy, is the spirit of gratitude. Folks do not appreciate things much. I guess it is because we have had so much, seen so much, that nothing excites us anymore.

I'm not speaking of him as a Christian, but I don't know another man in all history whom I admire more than Winston Churchill. Had it not been for Winston Churchill, doubtless England would have been bombed into the sea. I thrill when I read of that great moment when England was upon her knees and those millions in London every night were seeking the bomb shelters, as the German Luftwaffe were dropping tons of bombs. Fifteen years after it happened, I stood one foggy morning and looked over London.

They were still piling up the bricks, and the big derricks were still picking up the stones.

One day he was dictating to the lady who for many years had been his secretary. Suddenly he ceased to speak. She looked up, and he was weeping as he walked. Then Churchill made that famous statement that will live in history: "We shall defend our island, whatever the cost may be. We shall fight on the beaches; we shall fight on the landing grounds; we shall fight in the fields and in the streets; we shall fight in the hills." Then he made this statement, weeping, **"We shall never surrender!"**

The war ended. England, with the help of her allies, won the war. One man stood out in English history. He ran for the House of Parliament at the end of the war and was defeated. The people of England were saying, "The greatest hero we ever knew—we do not want him in the House," and voted him down.

Oh, the fickleness of human nature! How foolish one is to build hopes on people!

Do you know what the middle verse of the Bible is? "Vain is the help of man" (Ps. 108:12). God put it right there in the middle of the Bible. It's a fickle, fickle crowd. You had better learn this well.

If they had convertibles in that day, no doubt the prodigal owned one. His foolish father gave him his inheritance prematurely; and while the prodigal had money, he had friends. When he could say, "Step up to the bar; I am buying; they are on me," he always had a crowd around him. The girls flocked from everywhere. His friends were there. But when he had spent all, he wound up in the hogpen; and no one would give him anything to eat. The fickleness of the multitudes!

IV. MULTITUDES WILL BE JUDGED BY GOD

That the multitudes will be judged by God Almighty is the primary teaching of Joel 3:14. Speaking of the day of Armageddon—the day when God brings judgment upon the nations—it says, "Multitudes, multitudes in the valley of decision: for the day of the Lord is near in the valley of decision." Matthew, chapter 25, says these multitudes are going to stand before the Son of God and be judged by Him. Matthew, chapter 24, tells of the judgment of the nations, when all shall stand before Him. And when He shall come in His glory and the holy angels with Him, He shall sit upon the throne of His glory. Listen to it:

"When the Son of man shall come in his glory, and all the holy angels with him, then shall he sit upon the throne of his glory: And before him shall be gathered all nations: and he shall separate them one from another, as a shepherd divideth his sheep from the goats."—Matt. 25:31, 32.

Further on in this passage He says to some of these multitudes who are saved, "Come, ye blessed of my Father." But to multitudes He says, "Depart from me, ye cursed, into everlasting fire...I never knew you." Multitudes will be judged in the day of judgment.

Revelation 20:12 teaches us the same thing about these multitudes: "...the dead, small and great, stand before God."

> The day of wrath—that dreadful day
> When Heaven and earth shall pass away;
> What power shall be the sinner's stay,
> For whom shall he trust that dreadful day?
>
> When shriveling like a parched scroll,
> The flaming heavens together roll.
> And louder yet and yet more dread
> Swells the high trump that wakens the dead.
>
> Oh, on that day, that wrathful day,
> When a man to judgment wakes from clay,
> Be thou, O Christ, the believer's stay,
> Though Heaven and earth may pass away.

V. MULTITUDES WILL BE SAVED AND IN HEAVEN

I close by saying, not only will multitudes be judged but,

according to the Bible, multitudes will be saved. Revelation 7:9 reads, "After this I beheld, and, lo, a great multitude, which no man could number, of all nations, and kindreds, and people, and tongues, stood before the throne, and before the Lamb."

So multitudes are often mentioned in the Bible—some saved and some lost.

Which are you? Are you in the multitude without God? Or are you in that group that is wonderfully saved by faith in Jesus Christ? The saved of all ages, from Adam on down to the very last soul to be saved, will be there. They will be in Heaven from every clime, every walk of life, every color of skin.

What a glad day for the saints when we go sweeping through the gates of the eternal city of God! Jesus said, "And I say unto you, That many shall come from the east and west, and shall sit down with Abraham, and Isaac, and Jacob, in the kingdom of heaven" (Matt. 8:11).

"Multitudes, multitudes in the valley of decision: for the day of the Lord is near in the valley of decision."—Joel 3:14.

Chapter XVI

The New Birth

(Preached in Emmanuel Baptist Church, Pontiac, Michigan, January, 1955)

"Jesus answered and said unto him, Verily, verily, I say unto thee, Except a man be born again, he cannot see the kingdom of God."—John 3:3.

"Jesus answered, Verily, verily, I say unto thee, Except a man be born of water and of the Spirit, he cannot enter into the kingdom of God."—John 3:5.

Before people can become members of Emmanuel Baptist Church, they must meet with the pastor and board of deacons and give a testimony—a satisfactory testimony—that they have been born again.

I remember years ago a fine, well-meaning lady met with our board of deacons and me. When asked to give her testimony as to when she was saved, this was her answer: "I have always been a Christian. From the very earliest remembrance of my childhood, I never did anything wrong. I've always been a Christian."

That was not a good testimony. I knew, and the deacons knew, that in the life of every man and woman born again, somewhere along the line there must come that reality of the experience of the new birth, being born into the family of God.

The term "new birth" is not some phraseology that I have

attached to it, not some doctrine of the Baptist church. The new birth is the teaching of the Word of God. Jesus said, "Except a man be born again, he cannot see the kingdom of God."

Some time ago I was talking to a Catholic. He said, "Mr. Malone, you say that you must be born again. That's not the way we put it. That's not what we are told must happen."

I said, "If I could show you from YOUR Bible, not mine, if I could take the Douay Version of the Bible, which is approved by the Roman Catholic church, and show you that your Bible teaches the very same thing, would you believe then that it is in the Word of God?"

"Yes, if the Bible—my Bible, approved by my church—teaches that, I would believe it."

We took the Douay Version of the Bible, turned to the third chapter of John, and read almost the same phraseology I have read this morning. Even the Catholic Bible says, "Except a man be born from above, he cannot see the kingdom of God." That is the teaching of God's Word.

I am of the honest opinion that there are many people in churches who have religion, who have been baptized, who have joined the church, but who have not been born again. If Nicodemus were in this audience and, at the close of the service, were to come to one of our deacons or to me and say, "I want to meet with your board, and I want to join your church," unless the Holy Ghost of God gave us unusual wisdom and discernment, Nicodemus could join this church without being saved. You and I would never know he had not been born again.

A religious, good man was Nicodemus. The name "Nicodemus" gives us an insight into the type of man he was. It comes from two words: *nico*, meaning "superior," and *demus*, meaning "of the people." If someone had come into the community and said, "Show us your finest man, the very leading man in religion in all Jerusalem," with the exception of Jesus Himself, without a doubt, people would have pointed to Nicodemus and said, "There he is." Yet Nicodemus was not saved. He had religion, but he didn't have salvation.

Religion is what man does for the Lord—praying, reading, singing, giving, testifying, joining the church, getting baptized.

Salvation is what God does for man. Salvation is being saved by divine power.

Nicodemus had religion. He did many things for God. He was so outstanding that he had been promoted to a place of leadership. Church history says he was a member of the Sanhedrin, the Jewish law-making body of 71 men, who grouped themselves in the shape of a horseshoe. And the man who occupied the seventh seat was the most revered and honored of all, and that was Nicodemus, we are told. He was the leader of the Jewish law-making body and the religious leader of the nation of Israel.

The Holy Spirit of God mentions Nicodemus three times in the Gospel of John. In each mention, God says he is the man who came by night, who came after it got dark (John 3:2; 7:50; 19:39).

I've heard people make a guess at why he came by night. Some say he came by night because he was afraid to come by day. And there are people like that. There are people who would like to slip into Heaven by the back door, if they could. There are folks who don't want to walk down the aisle and make a public confession of their faith. They want to keep it locked up within themselves. They give this excuse: "I don't believe in talking much about it." They try to slip in the back door and come "by night" if they can.

Nicodemus might have been afraid to come by day. He might have thought, *If I come in the daytime, people will see me talking to Jesus; and I don't want to be seen talking to Him. Some will think it is a weakness on my part, that I'm getting religion.*

My friend, it's no weakness to be saved. It's just good common sense. Unless he has something to him, a weak man won't be a Christian, be laughed at, mocked at, in this wicked generation.

It might have been that Nicodemus came by night because he was a coward. Or he may have been like a lot of other folks—

"When I make a living, get all I need in life; when I get every-thing else taken care of; when the day's work is done, then I'll talk to Jesus about getting saved." However, I rather believe he came at night because he was busy by day and because he was a coward and didn't want to be seen.

There is something else about Nicodemus: he was a rich man. You know there are no rich men in this church. When I stand up here and preach, you can't say, "Brother Tom is preaching to the rich folks." Folks here this morning are all a common lot. But you don't have to have a lot of this world's goods for it to get in your eye and make you think riches have something to do with getting to Heaven. When the offering plate is passed, some people who are just as lost as lost can be will put something in and feel that it draws them closer to God. Not so! Nicodemus was rich but lost.

You know what the Bible says about riches? Read Mark 10:25: "It is easier for a camel to go through the eye of a needle, than for a rich man to enter into the kingdom of God." You can't buy your way into God's kingdom. If you give Him every bit of what you have, it can't get you one inch closer to God.

First Timothy 6 gives some important words on money: "For we brought nothing into this world, and it is certain we can carry nothing out." You will go out of this world like you came into it—with nothing in your pocket. There are no pockets in a shroud.

The Word of God says that they who love riches fall into a snare and are deceived by it. Nicodemus was rich, but he was lost.

Here are six facts about him:

1. **He was a righteous man.** Now Brother Tom, you're con-tradicting yourself. Nicodemus was righteous, yet unsaved? That's right. He was like all the Jews described in Romans 10:2, 3. They had "a zeal of God, but not according to knowledge. For they being ignorant of God's righteousness, and going about to estab-lish their own righteousness, have not submitted themselves unto the righteousness of God."

2. **He was a praying man.** If you had said to Nicodemus, "Nicodemus, do you believe in praying?" he would have answered you, "Yes, three times a day—morning, noon and night—I turn my face toward the Temple, like a good Jew, lift my voice to Jehovah, the God of the Hebrews, and pray."

One can say a prayer and not be a Christian. One can pray when he gets in trouble and not be saved. One can pray when he wants something very much and not be a Christian. Nicodemus would have said, "Yes, I believe in prayer."

3. **He was a tithing man.** If I had said, "Nicodemus, do you believe in giving to God?" he would have responded, "Yes, I do. I tithe my income." This man gave a tenth of all he made to God. A legalistic Jew, a Pharisee, obeyed the commandment to give the tithe to God; yet he was not a Christian. We read where he said, "I fast twice in the week, I give tithes of all that I possess" (Luke 18:12).

4. **He was a fasting man.** Nicodemus was a Pharisee, and the Pharisees fasted twice a week. In a few weeks we will enter into what a large part of the religious world calls the season of Lent. Some will fast, put ashes on their heads and think that it gets them closer to God. Nicodemus, twice a week, fasted. Yet, according to the words of Jesus, He was not a Christian.

Don't you see, my friend, how easy it is to have religion but not have the Lord Jesus Christ as your Saviour?

5. **He recognized Jesus as a miracle worker.** Nicodemus had heard of Jesus' raising the dead, opening the eyes of the blind and doing other miracles. So when he came to Jesus, he said, "No man can do these miracles that thou doest [turning water to wine, chap. 2], except God be with him" (John 3:2).

There are some people who have never been born again who talk today about the miracles of healing. You can get excited by seeing something unusual happen in a church service and still not be a child of God.

Nicodemus said, "Jesus, You are a miracle worker." Jesus

said, "You need to be born again, Nicodemus."

There are two kinds of miracles—miracles by the supernatural power of God and miracles by the power of Satan.

When Moses threw down his shepherds' crook, or rod, in front of Pharaoh and it was turned into a snake, Pharaoh, wicked and under the power of the Devil, said to his magicians, "Throw yours down, too, and show him a trick of yours." Pharaoh's magicians, wicked, unsaved, in the dark, threw down their shepherds' crooks, or rods, and made them wiggle like snakes and performed magic, too.

It's not a miracle you can see with your eye that men need. It's a miracle that takes place in the human heart, when one is saved, that makes him a new creature in Christ Jesus.

Nicodemus said, "You're a miracle worker," when he wasn't a Christian.

6. **He recognized Jesus as a great teacher**. Nicodemus recognized Jesus as a great teacher, but that didn't mean he was a Christian.

Now notice seven things that Jesus said about the new birth.

I. THE "MUST" OF THE NEW BIRTH

There's a law in the Bible called the Law of Prime Mention. The first time a thing is mentioned in the Bible, that is the most important passage on that subject.

Here is the first time Jesus sought to teach anything. Chapters 1 and 2 tell what He did, where He went, how He turned the water to wine. But these two chapters do not tell what Jesus said nor what He taught. The first time in the Gospel of John that Jesus opened His mouth to tell someone something, to teach something— the first formal discourse of Jesus—was this: 'Nicodemus, ye must be born again.'

It MUST be important if Jesus made His first lecture, His first sermon, His first discourse, "Ye must be born again."

There is not one other thought that could come to your heart and mind that equals this one in importance.

Have you been born of God? Have you been saved?

Notice something else. Jesus used strong language when He said, "Ye must be born again." When Jesus said, "Verily, verily, I say unto thee, Except a man be born again, he cannot see the kingdom of God," do you know what He was saying? "Verily" means the same as "amen." When we hear a preacher say something we know is important and from God, many times in our hearts and sometimes audibly we say, "Amen!" That is what "verily" means. Here is something so important that Jesus said twice, 'Amen, amen, I say unto thee, ye must be born again.'

No other way can one see God's kingdom. He said, "Except a man be born again, he CANNOT"—not MAY not, not MIGHT not, or PERCHANCE you might not, but, "Except a man be born again, he CANNOT see the kingdom of God." No man can see God's kingdom, no man can be saved, except he be born from above.

An eccentric queen adopted a little pig for a pet. She cleaned it up, put a ribbon around its neck, a ring in its nose and perfume on its hair. But each time it got loose, it took off and landed right into the middle of a mudhole just outside the palace.

All this disturbed the queen, so she called her private physician and asked, "Is there anything in the world we can do to keep that pig from jumping into the mudhole? Is there any medicine or operation or training program?"

The doctor said, "There is only one thing I know of. If I could operate, take the pig's heart out and put in a sheep's heart, it would stop jumping into the mudhole."

Do you sometimes wonder why you keep living in sin, why you keep doing things that are wrong? It's because you have an unchanged heart, because you have not been born again. To be born again means to be made new on the inside, made a new creature in Christ. And the only way one can have victory over sin and see the kingdom of God is to be born from above. "Therefore if any man be in Christ, he is a new creature: old things are passed away; behold, all things are become new'' (II Cor. 5:17). An old farmer came along and saw a bunch of boys at a spring. The water was muddy. They had dippers and buckets and were dipping out the muddy water and throwing it away, trying to clear up the spring.

The wise old farmer said to them, ''I'll tell you how to clear it up. Go back to the fountainhead, up where the water is coming from, and get the pig out. He is muddying up the water. Do that, and it will clear up in a little bit.''

So will your life. You will have victory over sin. You will see things differently when God imparts to you a divine nature, when you are saved by receiving Jesus Christ.

II. THE MEANS OF THE NEW BIRTH

The second statement Jesus made was in verse 5, ''Except a man be born of water and of the Spirit, he cannot enter into the kingdom of God.''

Chapter 3 of John tells us the means of the new birth. Two things Jesus said here: ''Except a man be born of WATER and of the SPIRIT, he cannot enter into the kingdom of God.''

Many think that to be born of water is to be baptized. Many good people tell us that. They believe it because their mothers and fathers believed it, and their mothers and fathers before had said to be born of water means to be baptized. They believe, when you go into a baptistry and the preacher baptizes you, you are saved, because they think ''born of water'' means to be baptized.

The Bible doesn't say and doesn't mean that. Jesus didn't teach that to be born of water meant to be baptized. If so, there was never a Christian until the day of John the Baptist. If to be saved means to be baptized, then all who came before John the Baptist were lost and are in Hell, because no one was baptized by immersion before John the Baptist came. That means Abraham went to Hell; that Jacob, Isaac and Joseph were lost; that everyone before

John the Baptist died in sin and went to Hell. And that is not true! If being born of water means to be baptized, all professing believers who have not been baptized are lost and on their way to Hell. It means every Methodist who hasn't been baptized by immersion is lost since he hasn't been scripturally baptized, but sprinkled. This is not the case. People in other denominations have been saved who don't even know what the Bible teaches about baptism. They are saved because they have been born again. They are saved because they have put their faith in Jesus Christ.

If to be born of water means to be baptized, then many passages in the Bible will have to be ignored. We will read some of those passages and see that "water" means the Word of God.

John 4:14: "But whosoever drinketh of the water that I shall give him shall never thirst; but the water that I shall give him shall be in him a well of water springing up into everlasting life."

Jesus said, "I will give you the water, the Word—the Word that I am in the world to die for your sins; the Word that by believing in Me ye can be saved."

John 7:37: "In the last day, that great day of the feast, Jesus stood and cried, saying, If any man thirst, let him come unto me, and drink." This should put an end once and forever to any doubt in your mind. Here water speaks of the Holy Spirit. He speaks of the Word in one place and of the Holy Spirit in this instance.

Never in all the Bible does God teach that to be baptized means to be born again or to be a Christian.

James 1:18: "Of his own will begat he us with the word of truth, that we should be a kind of firstfruits of his creatures."

First Peter 1:23: "Being born again, not of corruptible seed, but of incorruptible, by the word of God, which liveth and abideth for ever."

Now why am I spending time on this when I could tell you some stories about Mother in Heaven? when I could appeal to your emotions? when I could get everyone to cry? I could appeal to your emotions and maybe get a dozen or two to walk down these aisles, make a public confession, then perhaps not get saved.

This speaks of being washed in the Word of God. "That he might sanctify and cleanse it with the washing of water by the word" (Eph. 5:26).

In order to be saved, you have to believe what God has said. You must believe the Bible, the Word of God, which says, "All have sinned, and come short of the glory of God." This Bible says you are a sinner. In order to be saved, you have to believe that it teaches that you are lost without Christ, that you have sinned and are guilty before God.

And you have to believe that this Bible says Jesus Christ died in your stead, took your place on the cross, died that you might be saved.

Now, when He said "born of water," He no doubt referred to the Word of God—being "born of water and of the Spirit."

"Jesus answered, Verily, verily, I say unto thee, Except a man be born of water and of the Spirit, he cannot enter into the kingdom of God."

III. THE MINISTER OF THE NEW BIRTH

The minister of the new birth is the Holy Spirit, that unseen Person who speaks to people's hearts, who strives with them about their souls. Jesus says here that to be born again is by the power of the Holy Spirit: "Except a man be born of water and of the SPIRIT. . . ."

At the close of one service, a person said to me, "I didn't come forward to get saved today, but I felt like I should have. It just seemed like Someone was talking to me. I had an urge. It seemed like there was an unusual divine pulling in my heart. I felt like I ought to walk down the aisle and accept Jesus Christ. Brother Tom, do you know what I mean? Can you tell me what that urge was? Whatever it was, I resisted it, I rejected it."

I said, "Yes, I know what it was. It was the blessed Holy

Spirit of God speaking to your heart.''

Jesus was going away. He said, 'If I go away, I will send the Comforter—the Holy Spirit. And when He is come, He will reprove the world of sin, and of righteousness, and of judgment' (John 16:7, 8).

God sent the Holy Spirit into the world. He is in this building this morning. He is in my heart. He is speaking to hearts now. If the Holy Spirit is calling you to come and be saved, if He is pulling at your heart, it proves you are lost and that He is pointing out your need.

Friend, have you been born again? Does the Spirit of God bear witness within your heart right now that you have been born from above? Is the Holy Spirit talking to you? Is He telling you that you ought to be saved? Is He telling you that you ought to be sure about your soul? While He is speaking, will you come to the Lord? We are told, "My spirit shall not always strive with man."

IV. THE MAKER OF THE NEW BIRTH

God brings about the new birth. Jesus taught that the new birth is of divine origin. Oh, get that planted in your heart and mind. Let God drill the truth home tonight that to be born again is not something that originates with man, but it is of divine origin.

In John 1:11 we read these words: "He came unto his own, and his own received him not."

If one does not receive Jesus Christ, no matter how educated, how well taught, how refined, how religious, he is lost. Whatever he might have done, if he has rejected the Person of the Lord, he is unsaved.

Jesus taught us about saved people in John 1:12, 13: "But as many as received him, to them gave he power to become the sons of God, even to them that believe on his name: Which were born, not of blood, nor of the will of the flesh, nor of the will of man, but of God." How were they born? God tells us three ways these people were not born, three ways they were not saved, and three ways the new birth did NOT take place.

1. **"Which were born, not of blood...."** What does that mean? It means that you could have a Christian mother and a Christian father and not be a Christian yourself. You can be born of as godly a mother and father as any human being ever had, but that does not make you a Christian.

Remember, every child, every sweet little baby, is not as innocent as we think. Love is so blind. We can't see anything wicked about a little baby. But there is something wicked in him. The Bible says: "The wicked are estranged from the womb: they go astray as soon as they be born, speaking lies" (Ps. 58:3).

I didn't understand that until I became a daddy. An infant can tell you a lie just as quick as a grown person. I know two who pulled the wool over my eyes a time or two in their infancy. They will cry; they will bellow their heads off. You will jump out of your chair, frightened to death. When you hear him scream bloody murder, you say, "He's dying! I had better get to him and see what's wrong!"

Not a thing in the world is wrong. He will stop crying and get still to see if he can hear you coming. He is not in pain; he does not hurt anywhere; but if you're not coming, he will turn the heat on again. That is what Psalm 58:3 says.

We are born into this world with an Adamic nature. David knew this, for he said, "Behold, I was shapen in iniquity; and in sin did my mother conceive me" (Ps. 51:5). We were born as children of Adam. Every one of us has the same sinful nature. There is no such thing in God's sight as a good sinner and a bad sinner. All are born in sin. The Bible says, "But the scripture hath concluded all under sin, that the promise by faith of Jesus Christ might be given to them that believe" (Gal. 3:22).

You can be born into a family where there is a Christian mother and a Christian father, grow up to learn to speak the language of a Christian, hear the Gospel talked about, hear family prayers said, and hear the Bible read in the home; you can talk like a Christian, be religious, put on an outward religious formality, and not be born from above.

"...born, not of blood...." It is not inherited. You don't get the new birth from your father and mother.

2. "...nor of the will of the flesh...." You can quit all your meanness and still not be born again. You can quit every sin you've ever done, or try to; quit every bit of your meanness; quit your drinking and cursing; quit losing your temper; but the new birth is not of the flesh.

If you wanted to kill a tree, you wouldn't take a pair of scissors and cut off all the leaves. That wouldn't kill it. It would only make it grow more.

You can quit every one of your sins one by one, but that won't change you a bit spiritually. Man is corrupt from the inside out, and the sins a man or woman commits are only the fruits of a sinful heart. It's not of the flesh. It's not just cutting the leaves off one at a time. To be "born again" is to believe on the Lord Jesus Christ and receive a divine nature.

3. "...nor of the will of man...." The new birth is not brought about by good intentions and resolutions to do better. The new birth does not come by human persuasion. The preacher of the Gospel is not able to bring about the new birth. He only tells you the truth of the Gospel which, if you believe in your heart, will cause you to be born into the family of God.

The new birth is not by the will of man. No man can forgive sins but God only. You may will to be saved, but you will be saved by believing on the Lord Jesus Christ, not by your own will or determination.

V. THE METHOD OF THE NEW BIRTH

I want you to see the method of the new birth and see what it is not.

The teaching of Jesus shows that it is not reformation. It is not turning over a new leaf. You can turn over a new leaf tonight, but what about the leaves of yesterday? You can turn over a new leaf tonight and say, ''I'm going to be a new man tomorrow.'' But what about your past?

It is not reformation; it is not becoming religious.

Some of you will be surprised to learn that to be born again is not a change of heart. Nowhere in the Bible does it state that to become a Christian is to have a change of heart.

Sometimes people quote from Ezekiel 11:19 where, speaking to the Jews, God said, ''And I will give them one heart, and I will put a new spirit within you; and I will take the stony heart out of their flesh, and will give them an heart of flesh.''

But that is speaking of the restoration of Jews in the end time, when the Jews regather to Palestine and are converted as a nation. It does not refer to the act of regeneration.

You cannot show me one instance in the Bible where it says the new birth is a change of heart.

Then what is the new birth? What does the Bible teach that it means to be born again?

In II Peter 1:4 we read, ''Whereby are given unto us exceeding great and precious promises: that by these ye might be partakers of a divine nature.''

The heart in Tom Malone is just as deceitful and despicably wretched as it was before he got saved. Jeremiah 17:9 verifies that: ''The heart is deceitful above all things, and desperately wicked: who can know it?'' I have the same propensity to sin. I can do anything now that I could have done before I became a Christian. But I'm not as apt to, I don't want to, I don't have that desire, because I have a new nature.

As God looks down tonight, He actually sees in each of us two natures—the nature we were born with and, if we are saved, the divine nature which has been imparted unto us.

That is what Paul spoke about again and again and referred to in Galatians 5:17, ''For the flesh lusteth against the Spirit, and

the Spirit against the flesh''; they war one with another. That is
what Paul had in mind when he said, "O wretched man that I am!
who shall deliver me from the body of this death?''

Every Christian has the flesh; every Christian has the divine
nature. I am two people. I am a spiritual and a physical or carnal
man.

Every Christian is still in the body, and we will not get rid of
the flesh until the rapture. Any Christian can walk out of here
tonight and commit sin against God.

You ask, "Brother Malone, how can a Christian live for the
glory of God?''

An Indian speaker illustrated it this way: "If I had two big dogs,
one black and the other white, and I wanted one to dominate the
other, be able to whip him, subdue him, overcome him, how would
I do it? If I wanted the white dog to win, I'd feed the white dog
and starve the black one.''

Feed the spiritual nature, and it will be the dominant nature.
It will overcome, subdue and suppress the natural and carnal nature.
People will see in you the dominance of the spiritually new man.

But you still have the old man in you, in the flesh. God does
not take away your wicked heart when you get saved. God puts
in you a divine nature. Paul asked, "O wretched man that I am!
who shall deliver me from the body of this death?'' (Rom. 7:24).

People stumble on this point. When some get saved, they think,
Well, I'll never again do anything wrong. Did you yourself think
that when you got saved? I had a sneaking suspicion that I would
never do anything wrong anymore. Isn't it a shock when you wake
up to find that, even though you are saved, sometimes you do
wrong and sin against God and grieve the Holy Spirit? The reason is, you don't understand many times what it means to be born
from above, what it means to have a divine nature imparted to you.

God's method is not only to give us a divine nature but to
impute unto us the righteousness of Christ when we are born again.

"And therefore it was imputed to him [Abraham] *for righteous-*

ness. Now it was not written for his sake alone, that it was imputed to him; But for us also, to whom it shall be imputed, if we believe on him that raised up Jesus our Lord from the dead."—Rom. 4:22-24.

Abraham was saved not because he offered up Isaac but because he believed before Isaac was born. He believed in the coming of a miraculous son into the marriage of two old people. God imputed his righteousness unto him because he believed in the coming of the Lord Jesus into the world. Jesus said that Abraham looked forward by faith and saw Him. "Your father Abraham rejoiced to see my day: and he saw it, and was glad" (John 8:56).

When you are born into the family of God, He imputes righteousness unto you and sees you as in Christ.

"Jesus answered and said unto him, Verily, verily, I say unto thee, Except a man be born again, he cannot see the kingdom of God."

VI. THE MANDATE OF THE NEW BIRTH

The mandate of the new birth is authoritatively commanded by the Lord.

Jesus said to Nicodemus, "Ye MUST be born again." Why? There are two reasons.

First, everyone born into this world has the nature of his parents and is alienated from God. When I read such phrases as "Ye who sometimes were far off are made nigh by the blood," I realize that a sinner is cut off from God and cannot come into His presence.

An unsaved man cannot come into God's presence. He is cut off, alienated, separated. God told Moses not to let the people come to the mountain where He was. He wanted them to stay "far off." They were sinners until the blood was shed and applied and they had been forgiven. Far off. 'Tell the people, Moses, not to come nigh.' "And Moses alone shall come near the Lord: but they shall

not come nigh; neither shall the people go up with him'' (Exod.
24:2).

The sinner is cut off, separated. Oh, if the sinner could see his
predicament and his position before God! That is the reason Jesus
said, ''Ye MUST be born again.'' You MUST have imparted unto
you a divine nature.

Another thing: You MUST be born again, because the only way
to have life is by birth. How can a man get spiritual life? Only
one way—be born into the family of God. How did I get physical
life? By being born into my family, by becoming a child of my
mother and father. How can a man get spiritual life? Only one
way. By the process of the new birth, God imparts unto you a
spiritual life.

VII. THE MYSTERY OF THE NEW BIRTH

Let us read what Jesus said in verse 8 about the mystery of the
new birth. ''The wind bloweth where it listeth [goes wherever it
wants to], and thou hearest the sound thereof, but canst not tell
whence it cometh, and whether it goeth: so is every one that is
born of the Spirit.''

''SO'' is one of the most important words in chapter 3 of John.
Here the Lord is telling us that the Holy Spirit is likened in the
Bible to the wind.

There are some mysterious things about the wind. We may see
the results of the wind, but the wind itself is unseen or invisible.
So is the Holy Spirit. The wind moves sometimes softly, sometimes roughly, and no one can change that. There would be no
life without the wind and air. So there are no spiritual life and
no new birth without the work of the Holy Spirit. Jesus said you
cannot tell everything about the wind but ''thou hearest the sound
thereof.'' There is some mystery about the way the Holy Spirit
works upon the soul, but you will know where He is working.
Jesus said, ''. . .so is every one that is born of the Spirit.'' Chapter 37 of Ezekiel gives a most beautiful picture of the new birth.

There we find the valley of dry bones—a picture of Israel. God says to Ezekiel, "Prophesy upon these bones." He says, 'Tell those bones that I will cause breath to enter them and they shall live.'

As Ezekiel begins to prophesy, one bone begins to join to another. God told Ezekiel to continue to prophesy to the valley of dry bones. Ezekiel continues; and, lo and behold, flesh comes on them! But the bones with the flesh on them were still dead. So God told Ezekiel to prophesy unto the wind, to tell the wind to blow on those bones. As Ezekiel prophesies to the wind and the wind blows on the bones, these people rise up and live; and the breath of God (the Holy Ghost) sweeps over them.

Hear me, O friend! A soul cannot be saved apart from the work of the Holy Spirit. It is only by the Holy Spirit, likened by Jesus to the wind, that a soul is born into the family of God.

Now let me ask you, in passing, when you were saved or when you made a profession of faith, was it, as far as you could tell, a work of the Holy Spirit in your life?

A member of our church has wondered if one can be saved and not have the Holy Spirit in his life. I've gone over a number of verses with this fine man. As I read the Bible the other day, I read something, then said to myself, *That's it! That shows once and for all that not only is one saved by the Holy Spirit, but he cannot possibly believe in Jesus Christ and accept Him as Saviour without having the Holy Spirit come into his life.*

"But now in Christ Jesus ye who sometimes were far off are made nigh by the blood of Christ."—Eph. 2:13.

"In the last day, that great day of the feast, Jesus stood and cried, saying, If any man thirst, let him come unto me, and drink. He that believeth on me, as the scripture hath said...."—John 7:37, 38.

Friend, is that what you have done? Have you believed on Christ? As best you know how, have you accepted Him as your Saviour?

Well, then, watch the result of it:

"He that believeth on me, as the scripture hath said, out of his belly [innermost being] *shall flow rivers of living water. (But this spake he of the Spirit, which they that believe on him should receive....)"*

Jesus said you can't be saved and not have the Holy Spirit. You are saved by the Holy Spirit.

Jesus said it is like the wind. He and Nicodemus were out that night, standing under the stars. Maybe Nicodemus could hear the rustling of the leaves, so Jesus said, "Nicodemus, to be saved by the Spirit of God is like the wind. You don't know where it comes from, and you don't know where it goes."

Just as the wind is sovereign, invigorating, powerful, so is the Holy Spirit in the work of regeneration.

He is speaking to some heart just now. Don't turn Him away. Let Him come in, bringing peace, pardon, forgiveness and life everlasting.

"Jesus answered and said unto him, Verily, verily, I say unto thee, Except a man be born again, he cannot see the kingdom of God."—John 3:3.

Chapter XVII

The Night That Never Ended

(Preached at the Ninth Annual Missionary Conference, Highland Park Baptist Church, Chattanooga, Tennessee, November 5, 1957)

"He then having received the sop went immediately out: and it was night."—John 13:30.

In this 13th chapter of John, we find Jesus washing the feet of His disciples in the Upper Room. It is the night of His betrayal; it is the night before His crucifixion. In that Upper Room some wonderful things take place. They have met to observe the passover. As it was partaken of, there was a looking backward to the deliverance of the children of Israel from the bondage of Egypt and a looking forward to the Lamb of God who would take away the sin of the world.

Out of the passover feast that night, in the Upper Room, there came the institution of what we know as the Lord's supper or the table of the Lord.

Thirteen men were in that Upper Room: Christ and the twelve disciples whom He had chosen. As they sat around the table, Jesus said, "One of you shall betray me." They began wondering who it was. John asked Jesus "of whom he spake." Jesus replied, "He it is, to whom I shall give a sop, when I have dipped it."

In a moment, the hand that was soon to be nailed to the cross and the wicked hand of Judas Iscariot went together into the dish. Jesus said to Judas, "That thou doest, do quickly." Then one of the twelve opened the door of the Upper Room and walked out into the darkness of the city of Jerusalem and soon went to his death, the death of suicide.

Judas is in Hell today.

There are some wonderful lessons to be learned about Judas Iscariot. He is a most interesting character and has his place in the Scripture to teach us some lessons.

I. A LOOK AT JUDAS

Judas was not a Christian. I firmly believe that Judas was not a Christian. As amazing as it may seem, this man had spent three years with the Son of God. He walked with Him across the plains and listened to Him teach. He heard His parables; he saw His miracles; he slept with Him out under the stars at night. But I know Judas Iscariot was not a Christian for two reasons. Jesus said in this same chapter, "Ye are clean, but not all." One was unclean. On another occasion He said, "One of you is a devil." Never in the Bible is there any inference that a child of God is a devil.

Judas was a preacher. Yes, but that doesn't mean he was saved. You can be a preacher and not be saved. I have seen, in my brief ministry, a few preachers who were not saved but who came to know the Lord after having been in the pulpit for awhile.

Judas was not a Christian. Jesus sent them all out, including Judas, and gave them power over unclean spirits and power to heal the sick. The world today, and many Christians, have gone almost mad over divine healing. I believe in divine healing but not in divine healers. I would never have anyone accuse me of not believing what the Bible teaches on divine healing. I believe that God is able to touch an afflicted body and heal it. But just because a person claims to be a divine healer is no sign whatever that that person is in the will and work of God and is scriptural in his message and methods. Judas had a part in healing the sick.

Judas was guilty of the sin of "over-piety." I never saw a

Christian who was over-pious but that he sooner or later came to some serious trouble.

When a woman came and opened up her box of costly ointment and anointed the feet of Jesus, Judas Iscariot said, "I have a little speech to make. This is wrong. Here is a woman spending a year's wages on this costly ointment to anoint the feet of Jesus. This ointment should have been sold and the money given to the poor. This should have been used in the work of the Lord."

However, Judas didn't say this because he loved the poor nor because he wanted to give to the poor nor because he was interested in missions, but he said this because he carried the money bag and wanted the money so he could steal it.

I warn you Christians, you workers, you preachers, that the most dangerous sin of a Christian is over-piety—a professing of something you do not possess or professing an experience with God that you never had.

The worst trouble I have seen on the mission field or in any church has been caused by over-pious people. No immoral person could do much harm to the work of God. And everybody knows when a man is a drunkard. But when a person is over-pious and professes a spiritual elevation that he has never known—I have never seen it fail—this over-piety leads to trouble and contention in the work of God.

Over-pious Judas said, 'Why was not this money given to the poor?'

He had reached a prominent place, but he was not saved.

Judas fooled all the other disciples. When the apostles had elected Judas as treasurer of the twelve, they had confidence in him. He had completely fooled them. When Jesus said that one of them was going to betray Him, they began looking around that table in that Upper Room. Peter didn't say, "Yes, I know who it is; it is that Judas Iscariot." Rather, he looked at Jesus and asked, "Lord, is it I?" For three years Judas had fooled Peter, James and Thomas and the rest of the twelve. John asked Jesus, "Lord, who is it?"

Christians can be fooled by those who are not real, not genuine; but God can never be fooled. If you have deceived people into thinking that you are real, genuine and consecrated to God, don't forget that there is One who knows.

Judas Iscariot fooled everybody.

II. WHY JESUS CHOSE JUDAS ISCARIOT

You may ask, "When Jesus had the pick of all the men of His day, why would the Son of God, knowing men and what was in them, what they were capable of, and what they would do in the future—why would He ever choose a man whom He knew would turn out to be a traitor and sell Him for thirty pieces of silver?"

There are a number of reasons.

To fulfill the Word of God. "I speak not of you all: I know whom I have chosen: but that the scripture may be fulfilled, He that eateth bread with me hath lifted up his heel against me" (John 13:18).

He chose him to fulfill the Word of God. The Bible prophesied in Psalms that there would be one who would lift up his heel against Jesus and betray Him. "Yea, mine own familiar friend, in whom I trusted, which did eat of my bread, hath lifted up his heel against me" (41:9). A most wonderful thing about this Word of God that you and I preach and want to spread to the ends of the earth is that it says "the scripture cannot be broken" (John 10:35). Judas Iscariot was chosen as one of the twelve in the apostolate to fulfill the Word of God and make us know that this Book is truly the Book of God.

To prove the deity of Christ. As they sat around the table, Jesus said, "Now I tell you before it come, that, when it is come to pass, ye may believe that I am he" (John 13:19)—the true Messiah of the Old Testament, the truly anointed Christ of God.

So He chose Judas Iscariot to prove, among many other things, His deity.

To teach us the lesson of hypocrisy. There have always been hypocrites. In this chapter we see the difference between a hypocrite and a backslider. A backslider is one defiled by sin and washed and cleansed by Jesus. Peter got away from God and had to be restored; so he was a backslider. Judas was a hypocrite—a fake, unreal; he was lost, and he went to his own place. While I am in this pulpit and you are in this conference, a preacher is down yonder in Hell, tormented in the flames, alienated from God and forever lost—a preacher who went out preaching, casting out the demons and healing the sick.

O God, help us to be real and be what we profess to be.

III. WHAT "IT WAS NIGHT" SUGGESTS

Judas went out, and it was night. Mrs. Malone and I had the privilege a year or so ago to be in a room that supposedly was the Upper Room in Jerusalem. Whether it is, we do not know. A large room about one floor high off the sidewalk is said to be the Upper Room where Jesus and the twelve met that night. We sat there for awhile, thinking about the Lord's supper and Jesus and the twelve seated around the table that night. As I walked out the door and down the stone steps to the little narrow street, I thought of the night when Judas had dipped his hand in the dish with my Lord and then walked out that door, down those steps and out into the dark street. The Bible says that "it was night."

That suggests three things to me.

The darkness of the unregenerate heart. That night suggests the darkness of the unregenerate heart. More than a dozen times the Bible says that the heart of unsaved people is dark. In Ephesians 4:18 we read, "Having the understanding darkened, being alienated from the life of God through the ignorance that is in them, because of the blindness of their heart."

Unsaved people, whether in America, Africa or China, walk

in darkness; and their minds and souls are dark. They are children of the darkness, children of the night.

Those without Christ are in the dark. But saved people, you and I, have been translated out of the kingdom of darkness and placed in the family of God, and we have the light.

There is no more selfish thing that a Christian could ever do than to be led out of darkness into light and show absolutely no interest in getting other people out of darkness into light.

Because I came out of darkness into light, I know where I am going. Jesus said, "I am the light of the world: he that followeth me shall not walk in darkness." In John 12:35 He again said, "He that walketh in darkness knoweth not whither he goeth."

Don't feel hard at the sinner who goes to the bar and drinks. Don't feel hard at the sinner who dances and lives in sin. He doesn't know better. He is without God and in the dark. He needs the light, and the Devil opposes the work of getting the light to him.

"But if our gospel be hid, it is hid to them that are lost: In whom the god of this world hath blinded the minds of them which believe not, lest the light of the glorious gospel of Christ, who is the image of God, should shine unto them."—II Cor. 4:3,4.

Some time ago a friend told me this wonderful story.

A young Christian woman was on her way home from Bible school. On the train, she was reading the Bible. A group of unsaved men were on the train, in the same car. She could tell they were unsaved by their speech and smell—everything about them.

As this young woman sat reading her Bible, two or three seats down, across the aisle, one of the men said to the others, "You watch me. I'm going to make a fool out of that woman."

He walked over to where she was and said, "What are you reading?"

"I'm reading the book of Jonah."

"Oh, you surely don't believe that a fish swallowed a man."

"Yes," she answered, "I believe it."

"Surely you are more enlightened than that. That might be all right for the dark ages but not for enlightened, intelligent, educated people."

"I believe it," she said, "because this is the Word of God. The Spirit of God wrote it. Jesus said it was so, and He referred to it."

"Well, now, do you think Jonah is going to be in Heaven?"

"Yes, I think Jonah is going to be in Heaven, for I think he was a Christian."

"What if you get to Heaven and he isn't there?"

"Friend, I'll tell you what. If I get to Heaven and Jonah isn't there, then you ask him, for he will be where you are going."

Tonight you and I are in the light; but one without Christ, though he be a college professor or call himself the intelligentsia, is in darkness. God's Holy Book says, "For we wrestle not against flesh and blood, but against principalities, against powers, against the rulers of the darkness of this world, against spiritual wickedness in high places" (Eph. 6:12). We are in a battle. Don't ever think that winning people to Christ is easy. We invade the very regions of darkness when we seek to make Christ known. Thank God, we are in the light!

I'm not in the dark as to the coming of the Lord. The Bible says His coming will be like that of a thief. However, it will not be that for the Christian, for we are not of the night.

Thank God! I know the Lord is coming, and I've dedicated my life to getting the Gospel to every lost soul possible until He comes.

That text suggested the darkness of the human heart; and it suggests

The darkness of eternal punishment.

"Then said the king to the servants, Bind him hand and foot, and take him away, and cast him into outer darkness; there shall be weeping and gnashing of teeth."—Matt. 22:13.

Our text suggests the darkness of eternal punishment. Time after time God speaks of darkness as being typical of the eternal punishment He is going to bring upon sinners.

When God told Abraham that years later, down in Egypt, God's chosen race, the Jews, would suffer affliction and servitude and be slain, beaten and enslaved for 400 years, God caused a deep sleep to fall upon Abraham. In that deep sleep Abraham saw ''an horror of great darkness,'' the picture of suffering which was symbolized by darkness (Gen. 15). Jesus spoke of people coming from the East, West, North, South and sitting down in the kingdom with Abraham, Isaac and Jacob; but He spoke of others being cast into ''outer darkness.''

Do you know the people who need to do some thinking about eternal Hell? Do you know who needs to realize that Hell is a reality, that it is eternal, that there is no exit from it?—the preachers, the deacons, the church members. These should all realize that Hell is a reality and that every lost soul is going there.

A few nights ago my telephone rang. Someone said, ''You are wanted at the hospital.'' I went there to see a man who died later that night. Rails were up around the bed, and his hands were tied to the rails. I bent over to try to talk to him, but he was too far gone. No one had ever before asked me to talk to him. I found out later that he had been sick for a long time.

His wife stood by the bedside. I asked her, ''Are you a Christian?''

''Yes, I am.''

''And is this your husband?''

''Yes, Mr. Malone, and we have nine children.''

''Lady, is your husband saved? I can't talk to him; he can't understand. I would like to know if he is a child of God, for he is near death's door.''

That woman, mother of nine children, the woman who had lived with that man over twenty years and professed to be a Christian, said to me, ''Mr. Malone, I will have to tell you the truth: I don't know whether he is or not, because I have never asked him.''

If you believe that the man you work with is without God; if you believe that men and women in India, China and the islands of the sea are going to Hell, why in God's name don't you give your best to reach them with the Gospel?

One night I had invited a friend to preach in my church. I had the utmost confidence in him. I believe that, when he preaches, he preaches what God has put upon his heart. When he got up to preach, he said, "My subject tonight is going to be on Hell."

He preached with a broken heart. My heart was stirred.

That night a young woman came down to the front in tears. She took me by the hand and said, "Brother Tom, I have been a Christian quite awhile; I have been a member of this church for several years; but tonight I saw something I have never seen before—my lost mother, my lost father, some of my brothers and sisters, some of my cousins, aunts and uncles. Tonight God has given me a picture of my own flesh and blood, people dear to me, bound in the flames of Hell. Brother Tom, by the grace of God I will never be the same after tonight."

She is just a housewife. She has never been to any Bible school. She has never had any missionary training. But I can think of many a time when I have seen that little housewife come down the aisle, leading some woman or man and wife or three or four children; and in tears she would say to me, "Brother Malone, these are my neighbors," or, "This is my aunt and uncle," or, "This is my mother and father," or, "These are my cousins. I want you to tell them how to be saved."

Oh, may the Holy Ghost help us to realize that every soul who has not been washed in Jesus' blood is nearer to Hell tonight than they have ever been before.

I have a lost loved one for whom I have prayed for twenty-two years. The other day as my wife and I were talking about it, she made a suggestion to me about one thing yet I might do. I said in my heart, *"By God's grace, I am going to do that; and it's not an easy thing."*

Whom do you know tonight who is without God?

A man said something the other day that I can't get off my mind: "You are the only Christian somebody knows." How true! I will tell you something else: you are the best Christian somebody knows. Unsaved people who know you are a Christian wonder why you have never asked them about their souls.

The darkness of the grave without Christ. Years ago a wonderful man told this story. It sounded so unreal that I wouldn't believe it had I not known him.

He knew some folks years ago (he is older than I) who had one child, a little girl. They practically idolized her. That child had one peculiarity. She was always afraid of the dark. Every night when they went to her bedroom to put her to bed, she would say to her mother or daddy, "Now leave the light burning low. I'm afraid of the dark." They would promise to leave it burning even after she went to sleep. She would repeat, "Don't forget now; I'm afraid of the dark."

When she was about six years of age, she got sick. One afternoon, just before she died, the mother and father were sitting by the bed. Her mother said, "Now, darling, close your eyes and go to sleep."

"Now, Mama, I will if you will keep the light burning tonight."

"Don't worry, dear; it will be kept burning. Daddy and I will never let you be alone in the dark."

That night they kept the lamp burning as usual, but her little light went out. They took her up beyond the old farm home, upon the hill, to a country graveyard and buried her.

On the afternoon that they buried her, they came back home. There were just the mother and father, and the house was so empty and quiet. They were sitting around in silence and with broken hearts. The sun was going over the hill. All of a sudden the father said, "Mama, our little darling is up yonder, and I'm going up there."

This preacher said that the man lit a lantern, took it up on the hill to the graveyard and put it on the new grave. The preacher said that after nearly twenty years, he passed that way and saw yonder in that little country cemetery on a little grave a lantern burning. It was always burning.

There is a light in the grave for a Christian. There is a light in the hearts of all who know the Lord.

God wants us to send a light around the world.

"He then having received the sop went immediately out: and it was night."—John 13:30.

Chapter XVIII

Life's Most Important Question

(Preached at Emmanuel Baptist Church, Father's Day, June 16, 1957)

"Sirs, what must I do to be saved? And they said, Believe on the Lord Jesus Christ, and thou shalt be saved, and thy house."— Acts 16:30, 31.

Inasmuch as this is Father's Day, I want us to notice the record of the head of a home, the husband, a father of children, who got saved and, as a result of his salvation and spiritual leadership, his whole family became Christians. Immediately they were baptized and became a part of the church which was at Philippi.

The Bible teaches that God has ordained that a Christian man is to be the head of his home.

Man was created by the direct act of God. Woman came as a result of man. Even in the creative act of God, in the Garden of Eden, God says man is to have the place of leadership.

That is true in the church. God has ordained that men, saved and spiritually equipped, should be the head of both the home and church.

The greatest thing that could happen is that each home, if it does not already have it, have a man filled with the Holy Spirit and baptized with the love and compassion of Jesus to assume the place of leadership.

Here is the record of a man's getting saved and leading

his entire family to Jesus Christ, then leading them into the ordinance of baptism and church membership.

Acts 16 is God's record of how it happened. Here is a most important question which this father asked: "What must I do to be saved?"

Many important questions have come to mind, and I am sure they have come to your mind. One is, "Is there really a God?" Many have wondered about that. Is there a God who made me and made all things that exist? Is there a God to whom I am accountable, a God before whom I someday must stand? Now I have settled that question. There is no doubt in my mind but that there is a God, a personal God. I know Him as my Heavenly Father.

"Is there a hereafter?" Another question that comes to mind is, When a man dies and his body is placed in a casket and lowered six feet below the ground, is that the end of him, or is there a hereafter? I have settled that question in my mind. I know the Bible says that death does not end it all.

The biggest fool on earth is one who either says there is no God or who says, if there is a God, and we die in sin, that closes the chapter, and we never have to meet Him. The Bible states that man is an immortal creature, that man is going to live as long as God lives. Saved or lost, one hundred years, a million years from this moment, you and I will be alive somewhere.

Yes, there is a hereafter.

Sometimes the question comes to mind, "Is the soul immortal?" The Bible declares the immortality of the human soul. Jesus gave the record of the deaths of two men. These men were just as unalike as you could possibly find. One was fabulously rich; the other was pitifully poor. One was a Christian and on his way to Heaven; one was lost and in sin without God. But both died. Jesus gives us the record of their deaths but not of their funerals. People were at the funeral and knew what took place. The rich man probably had a most fabulous funeral, with beautiful horses drawing the beautiful carriage down the street and great crowds following. He was buried amidst pomp, splendor and riches; but Jesus records that his soul went to Hell.

"And he cried and said, Father Abraham, have mercy on me, and send Lazarus, that he may dip the tip of his finger in water, and cool my tongue; for I am tormented in this flame. But Abraham said, Son, remember that thou in thy lifetime receivedst thy good things, and likewise Lazarus evil things: but now he is comforted, and thou art tormented. And beside all this, between us and you there is a great gulf fixed: so that they which would pass from hence to you cannot; neither can they pass to us, that would come from thence."—Luke 16:24–26.

But the poor man, a beggar, who lay at his gate, full of sores, died and went into paradise and into Abraham's bosom.

The Son of God told of an unsaved man who died, and he didn't cease to be. In Hell he lifted up his eyes and talked. He begged, even prayed, in Hell.

No, death does not end it all for an unbeliever. And, thank God, it does not end it all for the believer. A poor beggar, a Christian, died and went into the presence of Jesus.

The soul is immortal—of course it is. But that is not the question I will talk about today. My question is the one this Philippian jailer, a husband and father, asked, "Sirs, what must I do to be saved?"

Why did he ask that question? Why would anyone ask this question? The jailer came trembling. Frightened and convicted, in earnest and with sincerity, he dropped down on his knees; and with trembling hands and voice, he looked at two preachers who could not be defeated and who prayed at midnight in the dungeon and cried out in conviction, "Sirs, what must I do to be saved?" He wanted to know, "How can I be a Christian? How can I be right with God?"

Why do folks now ask those questions? I have heard them and

so have you. I have asked them and so have you: "How can I be saved? What must I do to be saved?"

I. BECAUSE OF A DISSATISFACTION
WITH WORLDLY THINGS

Many people ask the question, "What must I do to be saved?" out of the dissatisfaction they find in worldly things. Just a few hours ago a man called me on the phone and said, "Brother Tom, I'm a businessman"; and he told me of his fabulous salary, of his success in the business world. "But," he said, "I have come to the place for the first time in my life when a good salary, friends and the things of the world mean nothing. I need help."

I took him in my automobile, and we drove around for a few hours. He had been on a long drunk. I met the people at the place where he worked. He truly was a successful businessman, the head of a large sales organization in Pontiac. We went to a restaurant, sat down across the table from each other and had a Coke together. As we sat and talked about what the Lord could do for him, he expressed to me the dissatisfaction that he had found in the things that had meant so much to him for nearly fifty years.

Many a person realizes too late in life that the pleasures of the world do not satisfy. Out of a heart disillusioned and dissatisfied with worldly pleasures, people often ask, "What must I do to be saved?"

I read this week what Solomon had to say about this world—Solomon, who had everything in the world that could make a person happy—if worldly things could make men happy. It seems that what Solomon said in Ecclesiastes 2:4–8 is so up-to-date:

"I made me great works; I builded me houses [sounds like the average man today]; *I planted me vineyards: I made me gardens and orchards, and I planted trees in them of all kind of fruits: I made me pools of water, to water therewith the wood that bringeth forth trees; I got me servants and maidens, and had servants*

*born in my house; also I had great possessions of great and small
cattle above all that were in Jerusalem before me: I gathered me
also silver and gold."*

Can you see it? Here is a beautiful house, orchards, a swimming pool. Here are the servants. Here is all the money. The man
I was talking to had plenty of money but no peace of mind down
inside.

Solomon said,

*"I gathered me also silver and gold, and the peculiar treasure
of kings and of the provinces: I gat me men singers and women
singers, and the delights of the sons of men, as musical instru-
ments, and that of all sorts."*—Eccles. 2:8.

Here was a big home, a swimming pool, servants and all that
money! "Now, let's have the orchestra"—and he brings out the
band and the orchestra.

*"So I was great, and increased more than all that were before
me in Jerusalem: also my wisdom remained with me. And whatsoever mine eyes desired I kept not from them, I withheld not my
heart from any joy* [I've tried everything]; *for my heart rejoiced
in all my labour: and this was my portion of all my labour.* [Here
is the result of it.] *Then I looked on all the works that my hands
had wrought, and on the labour that I had laboured to do: and,
behold, all was vanity and vexation of spirit, and there was no
profit under the sun."*—Eccles. 2:9–11.

This was a man who had everything. Yet he said, "When I
looked at it all, surveyed it, thought of it, there was no profit,
no happiness in it."

Oh, the pitiful thing is, sometimes men don't learn until it is
too late that worldly things don't satisfy.

Here is one who, out of the dissatisfaction of his heart, asked,
"Sirs, what must I do to be saved?"

II. BECAUSE OF THE RECOLLECTION OF
CHILDHOOD INSTRUCTION

I met a man the other day who had been to his mother's funeral. He had called and asked if I could preach the funeral, but I was out of town. Afterwards, he contacted me and said, "When my mother was buried, I began to think of her instruction and that of my father in my childhood—instruction I would not receive; the Word of God—I wouldn't believe; the Gospel—I wouldn't accept; the Christian training—I wouldn't let it have any influence on me. Now I realize that I must believe what my mother and father believed, and I want to know how to be saved."

I read in a Christian magazine some years ago of the influence of one godly man in the home. I read of two young men whose mother and father, godly people, had both passed off the scene. The father had a family altar in the home, as every father ought to have.

While the father was living, he read the Word of God and prayed during their boyhood; but now he was gone.

These two sons decided to tear down the family home and build two modern homes on the site where the boys would live.

As they were tearing down the home, the oldest son came to the room where the father and mother had gathered their children at night around the old-fashioned fireplace and read a chapter out of God's Word and prayed before they went to bed. As he tore up the floor and tore out the mantelpiece where the Bible used to rest, it began to move upon him. His heart broke as he began to recollect, and his memory was playing strange tricks on him.

He went into the other room and said to this younger brother, "Let me work in here, and you go work where I was working."

They exchanged places. The same thing happened to the younger brother. After awhile he went to the older brother and said, "I know why you couldn't work in there. I can't either. I have drifted away from God, and so have you. We have the memory and recollection of a godly father who reached on that mantelpiece every night and read that Book and prayed." Then he said, "God is speaking to my soul, and I want to get right with God."

They both got down on their knees and cried out, "What must we do to be saved?" They straightened it out.

Dads, if you live for God, if you have a Christian home, your children will bring honor to you. And if you won't live for God, you will see the effects and results in your children.

We talk about the problem of juvenile delinquency when it is a problem of parental delinquency. Where the father in the home will read God's Word, pray and exercise Christian discipline and love, there will never be a problem of juvenile delinquency. The Bible says, "Train up a child in the way he should go: and when he is old, he will not depart from it" (Prov. 22:6). When children go wrong, it is in most cases because something was wrong in the home where they were raised.

O God, help the fathers in this audience and the fathers of our nation to be Christians and heads of their homes as the Bible teaches.

III. BECAUSE OF THE ACTS OF NATURE

Sometimes people are brought to ask the question through an act of nature. That is what happened in the Scripture we read. There was an earthquake. It seems most everybody is getting tornado conscious. All you have to do is just hear one announcement over the radio, and it scares everybody to death. They tell you to get in the southwest corner or the northeast corner, and they tell you what to do when you get there. Yet there have only been two tornadoes in Michigan since 1875 that killed anybody or caused too much damage.

Every time there is a tornado warning, people get all frightened. A fellow said to me the other day, "I wonder if it wouldn't be a good thing if the Lord would send one of those tornadoes through Pontiac and scoop up about half the people. Then perhaps the other half would get right with God." I said, "If I were the half that was left, I know one fellow who would do a lot of heart-searching."

I might be blown away tomorrow or this afternoon, but I'm not going to worry about it nor run and crawl in a hole every time it gets a little dark during the day.

An uncle of mine nearly worried me to death when I was growing up. Since some folks had been killed in a wind, he built one of those old-fashioned storm cellars. He dug out a hole in a bank and put in a few logs over the top and covered it up with dirt. Little red lizards would get in that hole, but he wasn't afraid of them. Every time a little wind blew up, he would go down there and stay with the lizards and frogs and snakes. And he would drag my brother and me down in that red clay hole with him with the water so deep and lizards everywhere.

I said to him one day, after I had gotten a little older, "If I had my choice between having all these lizards crawling over me or being blown away, I'd rather be blown away. So this is my last time to crawl into this hole."

If I am blown away tomorrow, I know that such a disaster or tragedy will only usher me into the presence of God. And that surely wouldn't be bad!

There was an earthquake. God had sent it. And it destroyed the jail. When God sends a wind and it takes some lives, is God a mean God? No! As a result of that earthquake, in Acts 16, with the stones tumbling and people screaming and blood and broken bones and battered flesh everywhere, a man got down on his knees and cried, "What must I do to be a Christian?" Anytime it produces that kind of results, let God send what He will.

We hear so much about Martin Luther and how he became the father of the Reformation. Did you know that, at the age of twenty-two, Martin Luther was a student at a German school, and he was a Catholic but not a Christian?

While Martin Luther was walking along a road one day, a fierce storm came upon him. He was smitten to the ground and lay there while the winds blew and the lightning flashed. As he grabbled in the dirt, down in the midst of the road, praying for his life, he cried out to God, "O God, give me the Light that I might be a Christian!"

I say, if it takes an earthquake to make men cry, "What must I do to be saved?" then, God, send an earthquake that the revivals might come!

Yes, sometimes, because of an act of nature, men cry, "What must I do to be saved?"

IV. BECAUSE OF THE OBSERVATION OF A GODLY LIFE

Then many times men ask this question because of the observation of the godly lives of people who are already saved. I think that is what happened in this case. Here were two preachers who had been preaching the Gospel in Philippi. They had been thrown into jail because they had the power of God on them. A girl who had been bad got her life cleaned up in the city.

Paul and Silas were put in jail. Had it been I and some other preacher, you might have heard us say, "Well, if that is the kind of treatment we are going to get, we'll just quit." Had it been I, you might have heard some bawling, some crying. I have never been put in jail for doing good [or for doing bad either], so I don't know how I would react.

But I know what these two preachers did. At the midnight hour, Paul and Silas began to sing and pray. I don't know what they sang, but I know what they prayed. Surely, being who they were, they sang songs of thanksgiving, then thanked God that they were worthy to suffer for Him. "O God, we would rather be in these wooden stocks with bloody backs and on this cold dungeon floor than to be out yonder in sin and on our way to Hell, like that Philippian jailer."

As they sang, prayed and thanked God, that jailer heard it all.

Then when the earthquake came, he knew where there were two real Christians.

When the tragedy of life comes, are people going to look at you and say, "There is a Christian to whom I can go to get the answer to this thing"? That Philippian jailer saw two of the right kind, so he came and fell down on his knees and said, "What must I do to be saved?" They gave him this very wonderful answer, "Believe on the Lord Jesus Christ, and thou shalt be saved."

I heard a preacher friend tell of a Christian woman in the city of New York who wanted her husband saved. She prayed for him. She took him to a revival meeting. There, while the invitation was being given and while people were being saved, she turned to her husband and said, "I want you to be a Christian, dear. I want you to be a Christian father, a Christian husband and the head of a Christian home. Won't you be saved?"

"Not now," he said.

They went to their home. They sat down at the table in the kitchen. He was drinking a glass of milk. As he put the milk to his lips and started to drink, his heart failed. He set the milk down, slumped in his chair, and in a moment went out to meet God.

"What must I do to be saved?" That is the most important question that will ever leap from your heart and out through your lips. May God help you to think and meditate upon it and ask it today and not ever give up until God gives you the answer.

We are praying that many will come to a saving knowledge of Christ even as they hear this sermon. What is your decision? What will you do with Jesus? Before it is too late, won't you put your faith in the precious shed blood of the Son of God?

V. GOD'S ANSWER TO LIFE'S MOST IMPORTANT QUESTION

God's answer to this question is to believe on the Lord Jesus Christ. Believe in your heart that He is the Son of God, and believe that He died for your sins. He not only died upon the cross for your sins and mine, but He arose from the dead that those who believe might be declared righteous in the eyes of God.

Believing is something everyone can do. It is what you are to do in order to be saved. Faith in Christ is God's answer to the most important question that a person has ever asked. This is what the Bible teaches about how to be saved. "That if thou shalt confess with thy mouth the Lord Jesus, and shalt believe in thine heart that God hath raised him from the dead, thou shalt be saved" (Rom. 10:9).

"Sirs, what must I do to be saved? And they said, Believe on the Lord Jesus Christ, and thou shalt be saved, and thy house."— Acts 16:30, 31.

For a complete list of books available from the Sword of the Lord, write to Sword of the Lord Publishers, P. O. Box 1099, Murfreesboro, Tennessee 37133.